國家圖書館出版品預行編目

對沖人生路 自由價更高 / 錢志健著. -- 一版. --
臺北市：新銳文創, 2024.01
　　面；　公分
部分內容為英文
BOD版
ISBN 978-626-7326-15-2(平裝)

1.CST: 言論集 2.CST: 香港問題

078　　　　　　　　　　　　　112022707

血歷史240 PF0349

新 銳 文 創
INDEPENDENT & UNIQUE

對沖人生路 自由價更高

作　　者	錢志健
責任編輯	鄭伊庭
圖文排版	黃莉珊
封面設計	王嵩賀

出版策劃	新銳文創
發 行 人	宋政坤
法律顧問	毛國樑　律師
製作發行	秀威資訊科技股份有限公司
	114 台北市內湖區瑞光路76巷65號1樓
	電話：+886-2-2796-3638　傳真：+886-2-2796-1377
	服務信箱：service@showwe.com.tw
	http://www.showwe.com.tw
郵政劃撥	19563868　戶名：秀威資訊科技股份有限公司
展售門市	國家書店【松江門市】
	104 台北市中山區松江路209號1樓
	電話：+886-2-2518-0207　傳真：+886-2-2518-0778
網路訂購	秀威網路書店：https://store.showwe.tw
	國家網路書店：https://www.govbooks.com.tw

出版日期	2024年1月　BOD一版
定　　價	350元

讀者回函卡

A Hedge Fund Manager's Memoir
on the Dismantling of Hong Kong

THE
PATH TO
TRUE
FREEDOM

Exploring the Loss of the One Country Two Systems Model and
the Devastating Impact
of the National Security Law

EDWARD CHIN

A compelling portrayal of a Hong Kong hedge fund professional's unexpected transformation into a champion for freedom and justice. Ed Chin chronicles the fall of a once-free city now best known for its large number of political prisoners - a unique and dubious distinction for an international financial center. Chin shows courage and commitment in telling the true story of Hong Kong.

Mark Clifford
President, Committee for Freedom in Hong Kong Foundation

Ed Chin has been in a unique position, straddling the diverse worlds of financial markets, media and the fight for democracy and human rights in Hong Kong. In this powerful book, he shares his own experiences of defending democracy, justice and freedom for Hong Kong, in the media, through social media and in democratic politics, while working as a hedge fund manager focused on stock market indices, and he illustrates that far from being in conflict, these worlds are inter-related and inter-dependent. While in the short-term investors might be able to make a quick buck out of investing in an increasingly authoritarian, tyrannical and repressive place, in the long-run, without transparency, accountability and the rule of law – the values that underpin any open society and free market – financial markets get jittery.

Repression, the dismantling of press freedom, the arbitrary imprisonment of people whose opinions are at odds with the regime and the closure of businesses and freezing of assets of entrepreneurs whose views the regime dislikes, and the trampling of the rule of law and the independence of the judiciary, are not conducive to a successful financial market. In this important book, Ed Chin ties these threads together to describe the dismantling of Hong Kong's way of life, and the impact this has on us all."

Benedict Rogers,
Co-founder and Chief Executive
of Hong Kong Watch and author of The China Nexus:
Thirty Years In and Around the Chinese Communist Party's Tyranny.

目次 Contents

Preface／007

Challenges to True Freedom: Political Prisoners and the NSL's Suppression in Hong Kong／015

From Tiananmen 89 to Hong Kong's Ongoing Political Crackdown／019

Freedom in HK Is Now History／024

What Can Hong Kong's New Leader Bring to the Table?／029

The Upcoming National Security Trial of Jimmy Lai and the Erosion of Freedoms in Hong Kong／033

The Resilience of a City: Hong Kong's Fight for Freedom and the Mid-Autumn Festival／038

A Journey Through Time: Dr. Sun Yat Sen, Hong Kong's Struggle, and the Hope for Freedom／043

A Brighter Tomorrow: Hong Kong's Political Prisoners in Two Years, as We Continue to Pray／048

When Real Hong Kong Voices Cannot be Heard, We Will Have Nothing Left／053

For Freedom: Tibet, Democratic China, and Hong Kong／058

Remain Steadfast in Supporting Taiwan and Hong Kong／066

Erosion of Rights: Hong Kong's Dismantling Under Totalitarian Control／072

Hongkongers Must Live as We Always Live-Global Citizens／075

The Fall of Hong Kong Under the National Security Law／080

Human Rights Situation in Hong Kong Under CCP Rule／084

Standing Unjust Trials in Hong Kong／089

Leaving Hong Kong but Continuing to Tell the Story／094

Misplaced Hope for Hong Kong's Future／100

Hong Kong in Accelerated Exodus Mode／105

Remembrance of Apple Daily ／110

Jimmy Lai: Bravest Guardian of Hong Kong's Freedom in the Face of an Unjust
    NSL Trial／115

Preface

Over the past decade, I've authored ten books in Hong Kong, blending elements of politics and investment. However, following the 2019 Hong Kong Extradition Bill protests and the enforcement of the "Hong Kong National Security Law" in 2020, the profound political shifts in Hong Kong rendered it impossible to publish a book like the one you now hold. The "One Country, Two Systems" policy in Hong Kong has nearly lost its meaning, with the Chinese Communist Party failing to uphold its promises.

In July 2019, my final work in Hong Kong, "To Prosper and Stay Alive III, " surprisingly joined the ranks of "banned books" in the Hong Kong public library alongside its predecessors, "To Prosper and Stay Alive I, II, and III." In the era of "Patriots Ruling Hong Kong," the city appears to have regressed by 150 years, erasing the solid foundation laid during its British colonial past.

The year 2024 marks a period of significant change. I am fortunate to collaborate with a new publisher in Taiwan, continuing the spirit of words. The power of words lies in ensuring the passage of history. "The Blessed Island's" freedom is hard-won, and for most Hong Kong people,

Taiwan has long symbolized a "sovereign country" with freedom, the rule of law, voting rights, and civil liberties. In contrast, China's proposed "One Country, Two Systems" for Taiwan is seen as extremely perilous. Maintaining the status quo in the Taiwan Strait is deemed the best approach.

In the United States, the three major indices - Dow Jones, Nasdaq, and the S&P 500 - displayed a robust and highly volatile performance throughout 2023. The stock market, inherently unpredictable, saw tech stocks experiencing moments of both success and concern. Companies like Microsoft (MSFT), Amazon (AMZN), Apple (AAPL), and Google (GOOG) had already surpassed trillion-dollar market capitalizations, with Nvidia (NVDA) achieving this milestone in June 2023, its founder, Jensen Huang, being a Taiwanese-American.

This book, *The Path to True Freedom: A Hedge Fund Manager's Memoir in the Dismantling of Hong Kong,* aims to transport readers into a realm of imagination, delving not only into investment returns but also "life returns." It encourages readers to pay attention to global events. While this new book may transcend time, its main content will begin four years ago, in 2019. Reflecting on that year, it was marked by significant events, including China's 70th anniversary, the 60th anniversary of the Tibet uprising, the 30th anniversary of the June 4th incident, and a tumultuous period for Hong Kong. Following the Lunar New Year in 2019, the proposed extradition bill, often referred to as a "political bomb," shook the core values of Hong Kong. Millions took to the streets in the subsequent months, opposing authoritarian rule and uniting Hongkongers of all generations against an untrustworthy authoritarian regime.

Fast forward to 2024. Over the past four years, under the implementation of the "Hong Kong National Security Law," many Hongkongers have left the city to escape the Communist Party's rule. Some have found refuge in places like Taiwan, the United States, Canada, Australia, and the United Kingdom. The world's attention shifted to Russia and Ukraine in 2022, and by the end of 2023, the terrorist organization Hamas launched an attack on Israel, casting a shadow over the Middle East and global peace.

Barring unforeseen circumstances, this book is published just before the Taiwan presidential election. While I don't possess a crystal ball, I hope the new president of Taiwan can set a positive example for Asia and the world, demonstrating that a small population can achieve remarkable things with freedom, the rule of law, voting rights, and civil liberties. The ongoing political struggle between the United States and China, the potential return of former President Trump to the White House, and other political developments remain uncertain.

In reality, the true trade war has already begun, and capital has started to flee China, benefiting countries like Singapore, Taiwan, Vietnam, and Cambodia. In 2024, there may not be a "World War III," but there will be more complexity on the political front. From 1959 to the present, 65 years have passed since the Tibetan uprising. The events in 1951 when Tibet signed the "Seventeen Point Agreement" with China and the 1984 signing of the "Sino-British Joint Declaration" bear striking resemblances. In 1959, the Chinese Communist Party launched a violent crackdown in Tibet, and it has nearly succeeded in erasing the memory of the Tiananmen Square massacre within China's borders, leaving Hong Kong, Taiwan, and Chinese communities worldwide as the remaining guardians of that memory.

The 2019 anti-extradition bill protests in Hong Kong were labeled by the Chinese Communist Party as "riots," and by 2024, in addition to the "Hong Kong National Security Law," there will be further restrictions under Article 23. Essentially, Hong Kong's freedom of the press, freedom of information, and online freedom will continue to "converge with the mainland." China's economic challenges and Xi Jinping's slogan of "reunification with Taiwan by force" also present unpredictable outcomes. The world is divided into two camps: Western universal values of freedom versus authoritarian rule.

I've been involved in financial trading for a quarter of a century, and my commitment to democracy and freedom has evolved from a passive observer to an active participant over more than a quarter of a century. Under the National Security Law, many families, including mine, have undergone significant changes. My goal has always been to find profit opportunities through the leverage of absolute return techniques. As times change, those who don't understand the meaning behind artificial intelligence, blockchain, and cryptocurrencies will become out of touch with the times. What used to be called "illiterate" referred to those with low levels of education, but today's illiteracy is about not being able to use a computer or write simple code.

In the financial industry for a quarter of a century, fluctuations in wealth are inevitable. Property bubbles in Hong Kong and overseas have made many Hongkongers millionaires when measured in US dollars. However, by 2024, in a high-interest environment, highly leveraged homeowners have found themselves in negative equity, feeling unhappy. Different asset classes that were once seen as having no limits have seen property prices continually adjust. How many are willing to sell their homes at a loss at this moment and admit that their new home is shrinking?

One of the most significant changes in recent years is that Hongkongers have become "Hongkongers of the world" under the influence of the "one authoritative voice" of the Chinese Communist Party. We are now subject to strong surveillance and have lost our freedom of speech. Politics, finance, economics, and livelihoods are all interconnected, and the constant change in the identity of Hongkongers has given many people different perspectives, leading to adjustments in their thinking.

Absolute return is a game of strategy and tactics, and I enjoy participating in it. However, to be honest, after a decade-long investment career, it doesn't hold much meaning for me, especially as I enter the second half of my life. At the age of fifty, this "deadline" arrived smoothly for me over five years ago. The past is now behind, and new things are beginning. Financial trading was originally my main focus, but the upheaval in Hong Kong has given me a different understanding of my "mission" for now, if not for the rest of my life. Only when Hong Kong's political prisoners can "speak out" and receive support from around the world can the true story of Hong Kong be told.

The concept for this book, "*The Path to True Freedom: A Hedge Fund Manager's Memoir in the Dismantling of Hong Kong*," is to first discuss freedom and justice and then share insights into health and investment. Operating round the clock in the financial markets, both short and long term, and making the most of tens of thousands of days in our brief lives are the strategies and missions that define our entire lives.

The content of this book is primarily in English, with occasional traditional Chinese characters in the article, involving my perspectives on Hong Kong, Greater China, Taiwan, and global events. The content in the Chinese and English parts is unique in nature, and it will not be translated; it will be published as is.

I will dedicate this book to those who support freedom, ideals, creativity, universal values, and the courage to speak out on this planet, especially those who have been incarcerated under the National Security Law. At the same time, I want to dedicate this book to my mother, Dr. Doreen Chin, and my son Nathan. Thank you to my mom, for believing in what I do when nobody believes. And to Nathan, who was very young when the social movement in Hong Kong happened in 2014 and 2019, I hope he will pass the story to his children of how Hong Kong people fight for their freedoms.

With a quarter-century of trading experience, shaped by the unfolding reality of "Xi Jinping Thoughts and Emperor for Life," I've garnered fresh insights into finance, politics, economics, exile, and the intricate dynamics of being part of the diaspora community.

The transformation of Hongkongers into "Hongkongers of the world" is a stark reality. The prevailing sentiment among the majority is an unwillingness to accept that Hong Kong has been relegated to just "another city in China." Amid our pursuits of financial gains and survival, it's crucial not to lose sight of our initial intentions. Can we sustain our way of life without apprehension and preserve our distinctive culture? I value your thoughts; feel free to reach out to me via email at edckchin@gmail.com. Going beyond the realms of finance, safeguarding and passing on the core values of Hong Kong holds paramount importance.

Challenges to True Freedom: Political Prisoners and the NSL's Suppression in Hong Kong

I extend my sincere apologies for the delay in completing this article, choosing to finalize it on US Thanksgiving Day, a time I deemed fitting for reflection. As this article unfolds, the Hong Kong District Council Election campaign is in full swing, with pro-Beijing candidates actively canvassing. The election, slated for December 10th, 2023, follows the pan-democratic camp's substantial victory in the 2019 district council election. However, the subsequent disqualification of pro-democracy district councillors by the Hong Kong Government, combined with the implementation of the National Security Law (NSL) and electoral changes in 2021 and 2023, has raised formidable barriers for aspiring candidates. The 'three levels' of pre-screening, essentially pro-Beijing gatekeepers, hinder the democratic process.

In tandem with these political developments, Kwok Cheuk Kin, a lifelong member of the Hong Kong Democratic Party, applied for a judicial review challenging the stringent entry criteria for the race. Information from Mr. Kwok suggests a potential one-day trial around the end of November to determine the constitutionality of the current election arrangement. Sadly, recent developments, including Mr. Kwok being labeled a "non-registered voter," indicate the Hong Kong government's likely resistance to any legal challenges, seeking to discredit him and maintain control.

Furthermore, Hong Kong recently hosted the second World Global Financial Leaders' Investment Summit (2023), followed by the APEC Summit in San Francisco. Notably, Chief Executive John Lee Ka Chiu's inability to attend the APEC Summit due to US sanctions echoes the fate of his predecessor, former Chief Executive Carrie Lam. The aftermath of these summits prompts contemplation — did anything positive transpire from Hong Kong's perspective?

Regrettably, since the implementation of the National Security Law on June 30th, 2020, Hong Kong has witnessed a stifling of its people, an exodus of businesses, and the departure of HongKongers in pursuit of a better future. The extensive makeover orchestrated by the Chinese Communist Party (CCP) from press freedom to judicial independence, and free speech to national education, starkly contradicts the "one country, two systems" principle outlined in the Basic Law, Hong Kong's mini constitution.

The term "Lion Rock Spirit," symbolizing the resilience of Hong Kongers, has taken on new meaning. The imposition of the National

Security Law in June 2020 has prompted concerns about the erosion of political freedoms, hindering Hong Kong residents' ability to engage in meaningful election campaigns. The law, granting the Chinese government vast powers to suppress dissent, raises fears for activities deemed threats to national security.

On a personal note, as I sit inside a boba tea place in Toronto, Canada, on this special US Thanksgiving Day, I reflect on a poignant memory from 1985. The Cold War era, marked by a journey from mid-West Minneapolis to Chicago, watching Rocky IV, symbolizing the East vs. West conflict-a theme relevant to Hong Kong's current struggles.

Fast forward to 2023, and I find myself at a boba tea place in Toronto, contemplating Hong Kong's journey. Another war is being fought-the broken promise of upholding "one country, two systems" until 2047, with freedom fighters silenced, arrested, and unjustly awaiting trial. In November, the United States introduced The Hong Kong Sanctions Act, targeting figures such as Hong Kong's chief of justice, police commissioner, and designated national security judges. If this bill becomes law, both the Hong Kong Government and Beijing are likely to retaliate.

As the boba tea place prepares to close, I conclude my opinion piece. Since leaving Hong Kong on June 28th, 2021, not a day passes without thoughts of the political prisoners unjustly detained due to the

National Security Law. Perhaps it's a form of "survivor's guilt." During this Thanksgiving week in the US, I pray for miracles-for the freedom of Jimmy Lai, Benny Tai, Joshua Wong, and all those unjustly incarcerated. "Free Hong Kong" is more than a slogan-it's a cause we, as HongKongers worldwide, must passionately defend. May we all hold onto hope for a Free Hong Kong someday.

From Tiananmen 89 to Hong Kong's Ongoing Political Crackdown

By the time this opinion piece is out, we have a few days left leading to the remembrance of the 33nd Tiananmen crackdown of 1989. The political atmosphere is tense in Hong Kong, and with the imposition of the NSL (National Security Law) for almost 2 years, the city has tensed up, just like what is going on now at Tiananmen Square in Beijing. This year in Hong Kong, memorial services from the Catholic church will not be organized, and there is no more key organizer to the large scale candlelight vigil at the Victoria Park in Hong Kong. Lee Cheuk-Yan, Albert Ho Chun-Yan, Chow Hang-Tung, former chairs and vice chairs of the Hong Kong Alliance in Support of Patriotic Democratic Movement of China (支聯會) are all arrested, denied bail and waiting to be tried under the NSL.

Would communist Hong Kong be crazy enough to crackdown on private gatherings to commemorate what happened at Tiananmen 33 years ago, or to a scattered crowd who hold up their iphone in public with the light function on at 8:00pm? It will be stupid to see the NSD (National Security Department) or police start arresting citizens - not yet, I hope, but it might happen soon, as the totalitarian regime has been notorious for rewriting history, while trying to hide their mistakes and evil wrongdoings. But never say never. Cardinal Joseph Zen of Hong Kong, 90 years of age, was recently arrested under NSL charges on suspicion of collusion with foreign forces. This is the "new Hong Kong".

For those who don't follow Hong Kong news closely, Communist Hong Kong has technically banned the candle light vigil for the third time in a row - Hong Kongers have been steadfast in organizing the annual candlelight vigil at the Victoria Park over the years nonstop, which attract thousands of people, until the totalitarian regime banned it in 2020. The CCP (Chinese Communist Party) has now made it clear that any large-scale gathering is a big no-no, and communist Hong Kong's treatment of protest or public assembly is no different from the rest of communist China. Those who tried entering the Victoria Park in 2020 already paid a hefty price, as alluded earlier- the key organizers and well known supporters of the Hong Kong Alliance in Support of Patriotic Democratic Movements of China (支聯會) are either serving prison terms or are detained, something no one would have imagined even two years ago.

The detainment and freezing of assets of Jimmy Lai, the founder of Apple Daily, and a keen supporter to the June 4 candlelight vigil, has been international news for almost two years. Most of the outspoken voices for Hong Kong are either now in jail or are in exile. The hand-picked man from Beijing, John Lee Ka Chiu, who was a long time policeman, with the last two posts as Chief of Security and the most recent one as Chief Secretary for Hong Kong, will become the Chief Executive of Hong Kong on July 1st of this year. Hong Kong has definitely turned into a police state. Ironically, John Lee Ka Chiu is one of the 11 Hong Kong-officials who have been sanction by the US Treasury department under the former Trump administration, for aiding Hong Kong's crackdown and depriving of Hong Kong's autonomy and democratic process. (https://home.treasury.gov/news/press-releases/sm1088)

It is sad to see Hong Kong's autonomy fading so quickly, and the Tiananmen crackdown from 33 years ago has made another curse: Hong Kong, a city that once had supported the Tiananmen student movements in 1989, now faced its own curse and crackdown by the CCP as well. As a numbers guy, let me put this categorically in investment terms: CCP has abruptly issued "a put option with a near term expiry date to kill Hong Kong", and there is no genuine takers of this issuance, buyers or sellers alike. Whatever the CCP does now, will ultimately choke Hong Kong to death, and this is one form of mass destruction to its own city. (攬炒香港)

As for Hong Kong, the harsh political cleansing continues. Former legislators and district councillors who have been detained for over a year now, are hopelessly waiting for trial dates at Hong Kong's "kangaroo courts". The "confession sessions" are mostly announced through their Facebook accounts, which are managed by the detainees' confidents. This might not last for too long, as their could be further restrictions on the usage of social media in Hong Kong. We see a lot of similarities now between the prisoners of conscience in communist China and those in Hong Kong. The demands of Hong Kong people cannot be heard, and those who resist will be heavily punished.

The Tiananmen crackdown of 1989 was an indelible stain of modern China history. Former paramount leader of China, Deng Xiao Ping, was a man of controversy. After the Tiananmen massacre, people looked into this strong man with a different light. He came up with the idea of economic reforms, that attracted foreign investments. And with that, should come law and order that the international community would trust. Deng even promised after the Hong Kong 1997 Handover to China that "horse racing continues, dancers still dance, and one could criticize the CCP, and even if you do, the Party would not topple." Fast forward the clock a few decades later. It is quite obvious that the Deng's idea of keeping Hong Kong autonomous from the rest of communist China failed badly. The CCP now even "DQed" (disqualified), as local Hong Kongers would say, Deng's idea of keeping Hong Kong free for 50 years. And sadly, we were short-changed by 25 years of the so called "one country, two systems", and most people must have seen it by now.

I understand that we have entered the "new phase" of the "one country two systems" as the CCP influencers call it, and nothing can be further from the truth. Things get darker each day for Hong Kong, and there is no point in reminiscing old "glory days" of our past. While things look gloomy, and in the most extreme situation, CCP locks down Hong Kong, we should all continue to "speak very loud" right now. Let the world know about our situation in Hong Kong. Let us also fight very hard to preserve our core values- language, freedoms and heritage.

For Hong Kongers, no matter where you are, especially the political prisoners of Hong Kong who are wrongfully arrested and held behind bars, let's keep our faith in this uneasy journey to freedoms. The energy and spirit needed to keep the courage, hope and trust in check to keep fighting for a free Hong Kong is beyond what most people could comprehend. It has come with a huge sacrifice. It will never be easy to carry on, but we must have faith that better things are yet to come. We also pray that a free China and a free Hong Kong will come some day.

Freedom in HK Is Now History

Thousands of Hong Kongers pay their last respect to the late Queen Elizabeth II of England at the British Consulate-General Hong Kong, The compound is located at 1 Supreme Court Road, Admiralty, Hong Kong Island, which intersects with Justice Drive. According to the Wikipedia: "it is one of the largest British consulates-general in the world and is bigger than many British embassies and high commissions. It is responsible for maintaining British ties with Hong Kong and Macau."

My YouTube channel: Ed Chin World, and back up channel Ed Chin Voice has a freelance correspondent that reports on what is going on in Hong Kong. We cover anything and everything on Hong Kong live: from departure scenes of Hong Kongers at the airport with mixed feelings, to the recent vigil events to commemorate the Queen's death surrounding the British Consulate-General Hong Kong. To go up the consulate, most people will pass through a shopping complex called Pacific Place, and take the escalator to go up to the top "hillside", a quieter area in a rather bustling district of Hong Kong. In the past three years, Hong Kong has lost its glory due to political uncertainty and a harsh COVID pandemic policy, which needs no further explanation. People and businesses are leaving the once famed city.

September 19th, 2022. It is evening time in Hong Kong. and seven hours ahead of London. It was another work day in the former British colony, but a day of national mourning for the late Queen Elizabeth II, whose state funeral ceremony was captured by billions of people worldwide. The state funeral of Her Majesty the Queen was in progression. People in the UK and worldwide captured the Queen's funeral ceremony from all networks imaginable. At the British Consulate-General Hong Kong, besides laying flowers and pictures outside the compound and leaving personal notes to the Queen to show their last respect, those who came to the consulate felt a sense of "togetherness" and "belonging" when they mourn or celebrate for the Queen- in a group setting.

A middle age Hong Konger played the harmonica at the British Consulate-General Hong Kong compound area, with tunes of the national anthem of England "God Save The Queen", and also "Glory to Hong Kong", which is considered to be the unofficial national anthem of the city. The big crowd who came who paid their last respect to the Queen also joined in and sang the "Glory to Hong Kong", with lyrics in Cantonese. The 43 year old harmonica player, subsequently being identified by the Hong Kong police as Mr. Pang, was held inside a cordoned off area and subsequently arrested for suspicion of acting with seditious intent.

026 The Path To True Freedom

To come out in a big group is a rarity in Hong Kong after NSL The huge turnout of the Queen's vigil in Hong Kong also signifies a way of silent protest to the Chinese Communist Party (CCP), when China wants to completely re-write Hong Kong's history. That includes the authority's narrative of saying the 150+ years of colonial rule does not exist, and that the school books of Hong Kong would refer the British colonial days as "occupation a Chinese city by brute force".

With this NSL "evil tool" being superimposed on Hong Kong for over two years now, the deterioration of human rights situation in Hong Kong is beyond imagination: a prolonged nightmare, and bad news still keep coming. The very pragmatic Hong Kong people have speeded up their emigration plans, as there are more concerns of the new Hong Kong Chief Executive's administration under John Lee Ka Chiu will be worse off than his predecessor Carrie Lam. The rumored relaxation of the strict quarantine rules to 0+7 (no more quarantined hotel stays, but 7 days of stay-at-home isolation) is not a solution for international travelers and businesses. Hong Kong has lost its competitiveness, and "zero tolerance" to COVID pandemic is more politically motivated than one could imagine. COVID cannot be the only disease

Those in detainment already, like media tycoon Jimmy Lai, or some other highly recognizable names in detainment like young activist Joshua

Wong or legal scholar Benny Tai - whether they plead guilty or not - will be tried under NSL without jury.While the West is acutely aware of the torturing and ethnic genocide in Xinjiang, China, the cultural genocide in Hong Kong, the reshaping of Hong Kong's DNA by brute force - everything is more than surreal.

If Beijing is smart, the authorities should free Jimmy Lai unconditionally now. In fact, amnesty should be given to all NSL detainees. The Chief Executive of Hong Kong has that power, but unfortunately, it is not up to John Lee Ka Chiu, who is a former policeman who ride through the civil servant ranks in supersonic speed because of his "loyalty" to the party. Hong Kong will not be Hong Kong, unless there is genuine reconciliation with the people. We used to have a free society, an independent judiciary, and an open media. Beijing must understand that suppression is not the solution, and now with a political purge in Hong Kong, this barbaric form of gaining control in all aspects of society is true evidence on saying "one country, two systems" is gone completely. Whether Beijing want to rectify the situation, that is the real question.

It also sends a signal to all journalists and commentators in Hong Kong, whether it be print, radio or TV, which are broadly classified as regulated medias, or through "unregulated" social platforms like Youtube, Facebook or internet radio platforms, you better be careful on what you express, or you will get into serious trouble. As for the media operator, it becomes more and more difficult to form "alternative opinion" against the government, or their operating licenses could not be renewed. The days of being highly critical could be well gone. Ronson Chan, chairperson of the Hong Kong Journalist Association was schedule to leave this month for a 6 month fellowship at the Reuters Institute at the Oxford University. Now, for the strangest reason, Ronson was charged with obstructing police officers during reporting.

The totalitarian state is doing all the work behind the scene, and the citywide crackdown is still going deep and wide. As for as Hong Kongers are concerned, when the pan-democractic camp is totally wiped out, Beijing wants absolute control. Silencing all voices is surreal, basically penalize or even criminalize anyone that Beijing sees as a threat. I definitely see more turmoil in Hong Kong in the coming days, weeks and months. Let's defend Hong Kong the best we can, even though we all know the coming days will be brutal.

What Can Hong Kong's New Leader Bring to the Table?

July marked an unusual month for Hong Kong. Firstly, China's President, Xi Jinping, visited to inaugurate Hong Kong's new cabinet members. Chief Executive John Lee, a former police officer, was handpicked by Beijing for the top position. While initially shocking, Hong Kongers have grown accustomed to the city's absurdity as the "one country, two systems" principle has effectively transformed into a police state. Then, on July 3rd, celebrated novelist Ni Kuang (倪匡) passed away at the age of 87. During the annual Hong Kong book fair, author Chua Lam (蔡瀾) paid tribute to his longtime friend Ni Kuang, offering insight on how to approach death. Subsequently, the Hong Kong Film Awards saw 85-year-old Patrick Lee (謝賢) become the oldest actor ever to win the Best Actor award. Lastly, July concluded with a shocking incident as a massive screen fell on stage during a performance by the boy band group Mirror at the Hong Kong Coliseum, injuring two dancers.

Apart from Xi's official visit to Hong Kong, most of the news within the city has taken a notably "trivial" turn. It seems that trivial news has become the trend, with the belief that no major news is good news for

Hong Kong. Is this the narrative the government wants to promote, distracting the populace from more pressing issues? Hong Kong, which has now unmistakably evolved into a police state, has joined the ranks of Xinjiang and Tibet, characterized by the highest levels of surveillance and suppression. The dismantling of Hong Kong's societal fabric is surreal, and the new Hong Kong leader, John Lee, is known for his unyielding loyalty and compliance, executing Beijing's directives. After all, it was under John Lee Ka Chiu, a former police officer who later became the Security Chief and Chief Security of Hong Kong, alongside former Chief Executive Carrie Lam, that the ill-fated Extradition Bill was introduced to Hong Kong, sparking considerable grievances and turmoil in this once internationally renowned city.

For John Lee, who enjoys Beijing's blessings, his first month as Hong Kong's leader has seen limited criticism from the city's general public. However, appearances can be deceiving. Those in Hong Kong who once expressed their opinions or protested with resistance have either fled, been detained, imprisoned, or fallen conspicuously silent if they remain within Hong Kong. While the days of violent police crackdowns on dissent may have subsided, the government now seeks to further limit freedom of expression, religion, peaceful assembly, and association. It also seeks to indoctrinate the younger generation with patriotic education. This extreme transformation will continue until the city is fully "conformed" to Beijing's dictates.

As for the newly minted Chief Executive, John Lee, I hope he could distinguish himself from his predecessor, Carrie Lam, but my optimism remains guarded. This former police officer was rapidly promoted through the ranks of the Hong Kong public service since 2019 and his ascension to the role of Hong Kong's Chief Executive was unquestionably Beijing's decision. The position of Chief Executive in Hong Kong is a point of no return, and both he and his predecessor, Carrie Lam, faced reprimands and sanctions from the Trump administration for undermining Hong Kong's autonomy, along with other members of the current administration.

The million-dollar question is whether John Lee can heal the wounds of Hong Kong's people and set himself apart from his predecessor, the "most hated" Chief Executive of all time, Carrie Lam. Over the coming months and years of Lee's first term, rather than employing tactics based on fear to govern Hong Kong, he must listen to the voices of all Hong Kong residents, both those living inside and outside the city. He needs to exhibit humility and the ability to listen to diverse perspectives, which may be challenging given his background. The mass exodus of Hong Kongers due to political uncertainty and heavy-handed suppression has been nothing short of surreal.

What kind of leader will John Lee be if he merely holds Hong

Kongers hostage, as someone intimately familiar with the world of law enforcement, while refusing to tolerate any form of criticism? A turning point could arise if Hong Kong were allowed to hold protests or candlelight vigils for the Tiananmen victims again, but I understand this is unlikely to happen. The government can employ any excuse, however flimsy, to accuse its people of colluding with foreign forces, without the burden of providing concrete proof. This will only hasten Hong Kong's decline. If John Lee resorts to the "rule by fear" tactic, there is simply no way to revive the latter part of the "one country, two systems" principle.

It's worth taking a step back and remembering that both Hong Kong's police and some protesters used violence during the 2019 social movement. However, it was the government's excessive use of force and abuse of power that nearly resulted in a Tiananmen-like crackdown in 2019. If the totalitarian regime continues to make mistakes, Hong Kong is bound to reach a point of no return. Amid all the hopeful thinking that pervades Hong Kong today, I particularly wish that John Lee has the wisdom to connect with the people. Not long ago, during his one-man race for the role of Chief Executive of Hong Kong, his campaign slogan was "Starting a new chapter for Hong Kong together" (同為香港開新篇). My final piece of advice to John Lee is to listen to all voices, offer substantial contributions, and avoid becoming a greater disappointment for Hong Kong.

The Upcoming National Security Trial of Jimmy Lai and the Erosion of Freedoms in Hong Kong

In recent weeks, the world has been gripped by the brutal Israel-Gaza conflict, marked by its violence and the absence of swift resolutions. Thousands have tragically lost their lives, casting a shadow of uncertainty over the region. Meanwhile, in Hong Kong, a city once celebrated worldwide, a crisis unfolds as Mr. Jimmy Lai, the founder of Apple Daily, faces an ongoing trial. This trial, marred by repeated postponements, is now set to resume on December 18, 2023, all under the ominous presence of the National Security Law. Having spent over 1,000 days in detention, Mr. Lai confronts the grim possibility of a life sentence if found guilty.

The events of August 10, 2020, and June 17, 2021, where Next Digital, the parent company of Apple Daily and Next Magazine, faced multiple raids culminating in the newspaper's final issue on June 24, 2021, have cast a chilling and indelible shadow over Hong Kong's residents and those worldwide who hold deep concern for the city. The National Security Law (NSL), with its vague and ever-shifting "red lines," has created an atmosphere tainted by fear and self-censorship, erasing the cherished freedom of speech in today's Hong Kong. The stark choice between submission and punitive repercussions stands as a harsh reality apparent to all.

Apple Daily, which boldly declared on June 20, 1995 in its inaugural publication, "Apple Daily belongs to Hong Kong," intended to be a newspaper for the people, addressing a market gap just two years before the transition from British to communist rule. Today, Hong Kong is unrecognizable after the enactment of the National Security Law, with formidable forces seeking to silence free speech.

On another front, the stretch from the summer of 2019 to the present day has marked an unprecedented chapter in Hong Kong's modern history. People spanning various generations took to the streets, united in their battle for a free Hong Kong. It began with a million peaceful march, then swelled to two million all in the month of June 2019, all resounding in a collective message to Beijing: What Hong Kong people craved was genuine autonomy and democracy. And then, Beijing served HongKongers with the NSL a year after.

Contemplating these events, a pressing question emerges: How can law-abiding residents of Hong Kong exercise their fundamental right to freedom of expression and voice their grievances against the ruling government when the National Security Law has become an instrument that defies all reason? Over the past three years since the law's enactment on June 30, 2020, a series of disconcerting events during Hong Kong's profound socio-political extreme makeover has created a cumulative impact, compelling many to grapple with the heart-wrenching decision of whether to remain, enduring intense scrutiny, surveillance, and, at times, suppression, or to seek refuge overseas in pursuit of freedom and a brighter future.

The surreal events of 2020 and 2021, with hundreds of police officers raiding the Next Digital building, resemble a military coup, marked by barbarity. As someone who was a columnist at Apple Daily until its ultimate closure, I remember attending court hearings related to Next Digital as often as time allowed until I left the city in the middle of 2021.

In this "new normal," journalistic reporting critical of the government is no longer tolerated, and the totalitarian regime holds absolute unchecked authority to determine what is deemed "legal". International businesses operating in Hong Kong must now ponder the wisdom of continuing their operations within an environment fraught with the constant threat of detention and asset freezing.

Failure to conform carries severe civil or criminal penalties, including the freezing of bank accounts, venue closures, suspensions of activities, and staff detentions-an unsettling reality already witnessed at Next Media and online media outlet StandNews.

In these challenging times, it's essential to remember that the people of Hong Kong have faced numerous trials and significant moments as their city transformed in recent years. Despite restrictions on their physical freedoms, their spirit and resilience remain unshaken. With three years since the implementation of the formidable National Security Law, the realization that "old Hong Kong" has been irreversibly altered is sobering, leaving the city's future uncertain.

Nonetheless, the resistance to Beijing's growing influence in Hong Kong has spanned generations and brought together a diverse coalition. Students, professionals, civil servants, business leaders, academics, and journalists have all united in defense of their freedoms. Even as Beijing's grip tightens, the indomitable spirit of Hong Kong perseveres, both within the city and among the diaspora community of Hongkongers living overseas.

In conclusion, for those who have faith, let us join our hearts in prayer for Mr. Jimmy Lai and the six executives of the former Apple Daily, who were compelled to cease their operations two years ago. Let us focus on their upcoming unjust trials scheduled for December. May God send His guardian angels to protect Jimmy Lai and these six senior executives who now face accusations of collusion with foreign forces and conspiring to commit secession under the National Security Law. Let us pray for mercy and a change of heart among those in power in Communist China and their collaborators in Hong Kong. As Hongkongers, we yearn for a miracle for our city, and we hold onto the hope that Hong Kong will one day be free.

The Resilience of a City: Hong Kong's Fight for Freedom and the Mid-Autumn Festival

As I stood in a Chinese supermarket in Toronto, Canada, gazing upon the beautifully arranged mooncakes (月餅), I found myself transported to a poignant memory - my last Mid-Autumn Festival in 2020, spent in Hong Kong during a politically tumultuous period, a mere three months after the enactment of the National Security Law. The mooncakes on those shelves appeared to encapsulate the very essence of the festival, evoking a history of resilience and the compelling power of unity. This was particularly poignant when considering the historical struggles of the Chinese people against the Yuan Dynasty.

In that tranquil aisle of the supermarket, I embarked on a mental journey - a voyage through time, a quest to better comprehend the remarkable tale of Zhu Yuanzhang (朱元璋), the founding emperor of the Ming Dynasty. He was believed to have employed mooncakes as a tool to foment resistance against the oppressive Yuan Dynasty. However, it's important to note a precaution: some view Zhu Yuanzhang's story as folklore or urban legend, not necessarily historical fact.

This year, the Mid-Autumn Festival (中秋節), falling on September

29, 2023, holds immense cultural significance, symbolizing unity and togetherness. In this narrative, we delve into the plight of modern-day Hong Kong's political prisoners, drawing parallels to the folklore of the Mid-Autumn Festival and the strategic use of mooncakes in the Ming Dynasty by Zhu Yuanzhang to convey messages of resistance. By intertwining these narratives, we aim to highlight the unwavering resilience of Hong Kong's democracy movement and its relentless pursuit of freedom in the face of oppression.

Zhu Yuanzhang, the visionary founding emperor of the Ming Dynasty, emerged as a beacon of resistance during the 14th century, confronting the oppressive rule of the Yuan Dynasty. Facing an era of suppression, Zhu Yuanzhang orchestrated a rebellion to restore Han Chinese rule, overcoming monumental challenges in organizing resistance efforts and disseminating information. During these turbulent times, he ingeniously turned to the Mid-Autumn Festival as a strategic tool.

In this tumultuous period, mooncakes played a pivotal role in conveying critical information. Zhu Yuanzhang and his rebels utilized mooncakes as a means to clandestinely spread messages among the Han Chinese populace, who were largely disenchanted with the Mongol rule. Concealed within these pastries were small pieces of paper containing crucial instructions and rallying cries, effectively disguising their revolutionary plans.

During the 13th century, communication was heavily controlled by the Yuan Dynasty. Rebel leaders recognized the necessity for a covert method to disseminate information widely. Mooncakes, widely consumed during the Mid-Autumn Festival, provided the perfect medium for this purpose. Rebels distributed mooncakes containing hidden messages, encouraging the people to unite against their oppressive rulers.

Fast-forwarding to modern times, Hong Kong's fight for freedom intensified during the 2019 anti-extradition movement. The movement united people of all ages and backgrounds, showcasing their determination to protect their autonomy and resist Beijing's encroachments on their freedoms. The "one country, two systems" principle was gradually eroding, prompting widespread protests and strikes.

The mooncakes, with their symbolic round shape, also represent unity and togetherness. For the diaspora community, this symbol carries even more weight. It signifies their shared struggle for freedom and the unity needed to navigate the challenges they face in their new environments. Just as the mooncakes bring families together, they remind the diaspora of the unity and solidarity they must maintain in their fight for Hong Kong's glory.

In the wake of the 2019 anti-extradition law resistance in Hong

Kong, the enactment of the National Security Law in June 2020 marked a turning point, prompting an exodus of Hong Kongers seeking refuge and freedom abroad. This mass migration has led to a significant growth in the diaspora community of Hong Kongers overseas. As the Mid-Autumn Festival approaches, a tradition where families gather to enjoy mooncakes and celebrate, it is a poignant moment for many in the diaspora community. The mooncakes, a symbol of unity and togetherness, evoke memories of the good old glory days of Hong Kong.

Hong Kong's resistance against the increasing influence of Beijing was cross-generational and diverse. From students to professionals, from civil servants to business people, and from academics to journalists, they stood together to safeguard their liberties. Despite the tightening grip of Beijing, Hong Kong's resilience remained unwavering, mirroring the spirit of defiance seen in Zhu Yuanzhang's era.

Amidst this struggle for freedom, numerous individuals found themselves imprisoned, enduring the loss of liberties. Notably, Jimmy Lai (黎智英), the founder of Apple Daily, marked his 1000th day of incarceration on September 26, 2023, under the National Security Law. Inside the Hong Kong jails, prisoners, including political ones, received mini mooncakes during the Mid-Autumn Festival. This small token symbolized hope and a reminder that even in confinement, the quest for freedom persisted.

In conclusion, the folklore of Zhu Yuanzhang and the strategic use of mooncakes as a means of resistance resonate with Hong Kong's modern-day fight for freedom. The Mid-Autumn Festival, celebrated with mooncakes, is a time to remember the struggles of the past and appreciate the present. Despite the centuries that separate these events, the pursuit of freedom stands as an influential, unifying element, showcasing humanity's unwavering spirit. Hong Kong's battle for autonomy and democracy stands as a testament to the enduring strength of both a city and its populace. The Hong Kong diaspora must persist in expressing their beliefs and standing with those who sacrificed their freedoms for a greater ideal. The faith in a liberated Hong Kong persists, residing in the hearts and actions of those who hold freedom dear. Let us cling to hope, for a free Hong Kong shall rise again. And to those reveling in the festivities, may your mid-Autumn festival be joyous and fulfilling.

A Journey Through Time: Dr. Sun Yat Sen, Hong Kong's Struggle, and the Hope for Freedom

In June of 2021, just days before I embarked on a one-way Air Canada flight, I stood on the threshold of the Dr. Sun Yat Sen Museum (孫中山紀念館) in mid-level Hong Kong. The museum was a mere 10-minute walk from my office in Central, yet it felt like a portal to another era, a time capsule that transported me 140 years into the past. It was a poignant moment of reflection, a chance to delve deep into history, and a vivid reminder of the relentless struggle for freedom and democracy in Hong Kong.

The Dr. Sun Yat Sen Museum serves as a testament to the life and legacy of Dr. Sun Yat Sen, often hailed as the father of modern China. His significance is indisputable, with both communist China and Taiwan honoring his memory. As I wandered through the museum's exhibits, I was reminded that Dr. Sun's formative years were spent in Hong Kong. He attended the prestigious Diocesan Boys' School (拔萃男書院), my own alma mater, and pursued his medical studies at what is now Hong Kong University (香港大學).

It was during his time in Hong Kong that Dr. Sun began to formulate his revolutionary ideas, ideas that would go on to change the course of history. I couldn't help but marvel at the profound impact of this city on a young man's life, a man who would eventually become one of the most influential figures in modern Chinese history.

My visit to the museum wasn't just a journey through Dr. Sun's life, but also a voyage through China's tumultuous history. I closed my eyes and envisioned myself witnessing the chaos and upheaval of China's civil war, the fall of the Qing Dynasty, and the birth of a new China. I traveled through time, from those early revolutionary days to the present, where China stands as a dangerous superpower under the rule of authoritarian leader Xi Jinping. The oppression extends beyond mainland China to Hong Kong, where the autonomy promised under the "one country, two systems" framework has been undermined through the imposition of the National Security Law.

Once again, as I immersed myself in Dr. Sun's world, I couldn't help but wonder how he, as a young revolutionary, had navigated the treacherous waters of Imperial China and the oppressive Qing Dynasty. It was a time when the mere act of advocating for reform was a dangerous endeavor, yet Dr. Sun's unwavering determination and vision for a reformed China led him down a path that would change history.

In my mind's eye, I saw Dr. Sun's struggle mirrored in the modern-day fight for freedom in Hong Kong. The year 2019 marked a pivotal moment in the city's history, as Hong Kongers united in their resistance against Beijing's encroachment on their promised freedoms under "one country, two systems." The infamous extradition bill became a symbol of this struggle, and the city's people took to the streets, echoing Dr. Sun's call for reform over a century earlier.

However, the fight had taken a toll. More than 200 political prisoners remained in detention, awaiting an uncertain fate in Hong Kong's increasingly flawed judicial system. Many had chosen to leave their birthplace, seeking refuge in countries like Canada, the United Kingdom, and Australia. As a global citizen, I was acutely aware of the unjust trials faced by figures like Jimmy Lai (黎智英), Benny Tai (戴耀廷), and Joshua Wong (黃之鋒), individuals who had become symbols of Hong Kong's resilience.

Organizations like Hong Kong Watch, the Hong Kong Democracy Council, and the Committee of Freedom for Hong Kong tirelessly monitored the situation of these political prisoners. Meanwhile, influential voices on various YouTube channels played a crucial role in raising global awareness about Hong Kong's plight, serving as a critical check and balance in these tumultuous times.

In the present day, especially after the enactment of the National Security Law (NSL) in mid-2020, Hong Kong's top activists from various backgrounds found themselves in the midst of court trials. This was a juncture where the international community needed to unite in condemnation of communist China and Hong Kong for undermining the city's once-famed autonomy.

One striking example was the delayed trial of Jimmy Lai, the former publisher, and founder of Apple Daily newspaper. The NSL had been weaponized to extinguish fair trials in Hong Kong, eroding the independence of the judiciary and driving away foreign investments due to political uncertainty.

Amidst these challenges, I found myself grappling with a mix of emotions. The future looked bleak, and yet, history had shown us that miracles were possible. Apartheid had ended in South Africa, and East and West Germany had reunited in 1990. These were moments when the world had witnessed the triumph of hope and resilience.

As I left the museum that day in June of 2021, I carried with me a renewed sense of purpose. Dr. Sun Yat Sen's legacy lived on, a testament to the enduring struggle for freedom and democracy. It was a legacy that would inspire me to advocate for a day when Hong Kong would once again stand as a beacon of hope and "one country, two systems" would regain its true meaning.

In conclusion, my visit to the Dr. Sun Yat Sen Museum was a profound and emotional experience. It served as a stark reminder of the struggles endured in the past and the challenges faced in the present. Dr. Sun's legacy transcended time, and I remained hopeful that Hong Kong would one day reclaim its autonomy and become a symbol of freedom once more.

A Brighter Tomorrow: Hong Kong's Political Prisoners in Two Years, as We Continue to Pray

As we approach the end of August, my mind is filled with thoughts of Hong Kong. This city has experienced significant changes due to the strict National Security Law (NSL) imposed by Beijing. In early September, my team will host the "Global Prayer Movement for Hong Kong's Political Prisoners" as part of the three day "World Hong Kong Forum" in Toronto Canada, which I'll elaborate in this month's written piece.

In this August commentary, I want to take you on an imaginative journey into the future. I'll try to predict what might happen to the political prisoners in Hong Kong, focusing on my dear friends Jimmy Lai, Benny Tai, and Joshua Wong, who are now unjustly imprisoned due to the NSL.

As a Christian, I find comfort in prayer. I pray fervently for the release of Jimmy Lai, Benny Tai, Joshua Wong, and the more than 200 other political prisoners. I firmly believe that their suffering will not be in vain. I also dare to make a prediction: there might be a "prisoner swap" involving Jimmy Lai, Benny Tai, Joshua Wong, and others with some of the most wanted individuals from the Chinese Communist Party.

Now, let's look ahead to 2025. The situation in Hong Kong appears grim. The city's status as a major international financial center has declined due to the NSL. Many international investment banks have relocated their key personnel to other Asian countries like Japan, Singapore, and Taiwan.

The NSL, implemented by Beijing in 2020, has become a tool of mass suppression. It criminalizes various activities related to secession, subversion, terrorism, and collusion with foreign forces, casting a dark shadow over Hong Kong's democratic aspirations. In this context, activists from Hong Kong who are now in other countries continue to lobby the European Union, United States, United Kingdom, and Canada for further sanctions against Beijing and Hong Kong officials due to human rights violations.

In this future scenario, my friends remain detained or serving prison terms under the NSL. Jimmy Lai, the founder of Next Digital and a vocal critic of Beijing's policies, was arrested in August 2020 and has faced numerous charges since. Benny Tai, a prominent legal scholar involved in the 2014 Umbrella Movement, was arrested in April 2020 and has sought solace in reading the Bible and autobiographies like Nelson Mandela's "Long Walk to Freedom." Joshua Wong, known for his youthful activism, faces charges related to unauthorized assemblies and protest coordination.

Looking to 2025, the path for political prisoners in Hong Kong appears uncertain. The city's democratic values seem to be fading away, and more foreign firms have left. The Hong Kong dollar's peg to the US dollar is under significant pressure, with hedge fund speculators betting on its devaluation.

By 2025, Hong Kong's political situation has deteriorated further. Beijing's control over the city has tightened dramatically, leading to a climate of fear. The National Security Police now have more authority and are making arbitrary arrests, resembling the oppressive world depicted in George Orwell's "1984."

People are afraid to express their opinions, fearing arrest by the authorities. Hong Kong, once known for its freedoms, has seen those freedoms erode. The legal system, once impartial, is now influenced by politics, making it difficult to find justice for those unfairly treated. The future for Hong Kong appears uncertain and troubling in 2025, with people living in fear. Despite these challenges, they hold onto hope that things will improve.

The global response to China's actions in Hong Kong remains crucial. By 2025, international pressure to secure the release of political prisoners may have grown stronger. Nations may use diplomatic tools, more forceful sanctions, and collective calls for action to persuade

China to respect human rights. The strength of this global outcry could determine the fate of the prisoners.

The political prisoners in Hong Kong are unlikely to give up. In 2025, they may continue challenging their detention under the National Security Law, invoking international human rights standards and Hong Kong's Basic Law. The NSL has given extensive powers to National Security Judges who might continue conducting unfair trials. This means that seeking justice will be tough. However, these political prisoners won't be alone in this fight. The global community, human rights organizations, and supporters from around the world will continue to stand by them. The international outcry against the loss of freedoms in Hong Kong will grow louder.

As a Christian, I find solace in prayer, believing that faith can overcome even the darkest times. I pray daily for the freedom and well-being of my friends – Jimmy Lai, Benny Tai, and Joshua Wong. Amid the shadows, I hold onto the belief that their suffering will not be in vain. I trust that justice will prevail, paving the way for a better Hong Kong.

As we look into the future of political prisoners in Hong Kong in 2025, our hearts are filled with empathy and a strong desire for justice. The contrast between Hong Kong's past as a bastion of democracy and its current reality under Chief Executive John Lee and Security Chief Chris

Tang is a stark reminder of the ongoing struggle for freedom.

My close friends, Jimmy Lai, Benny Tai, and Joshua Wong, who were once symbols of hope, have evolved into something even greater. Their Christian faith and their positive approach to suffering have elevated them to a more spiritual level. Now, they embody the unyielding spirit of those who won't give in to tyranny. Their sacrifices serve as a powerful reminder that even in the bleakest times, the human spirit can radiate brightly. Let the world witness their unwavering strength, and let the voices of the oppressed keep resounding, undaunted by the pressures of oppression. We also pray that a free Hong Kong will come someday.

When Real Hong Kong Voices Cannot be Heard, We Will Have Nothing Left

It has been a long journey, to see the extreme transformation of Hong Kong: past, present and a definite more uncertain future. Since the enactment of the National Security Law (NSL) in Hong Kong more than three years ago, HongKongers have been in an exodus mode. Those who stay behind, have lost their rights to free speech. And for those living in the city have to live under fear. The NSL was the start of a nightmare that leads to the present day.

The latest blow to Hong Kong, was that the communist Hong Kong government issued a bounty, HKD 1 million each, around USD 128K per person, to the heads of 8 Hong Kong activists from various backgrounds who are now overseas. The communist Hong Kong government says they will "hunt them down till the ends of the earth", but those officials who made these wild statements, ironically, have been on the US government sanction list, for destroying Hong Kong's autonomy. But what is worst, the national security police also interfere with the related persons of the "Hong Kong 8": their sons and daughters, mothers and fathers or siblings. Elmer Yuen, a "senior activist" by age and in his 70s, has also witnessed

054 The Path To True Freedom

his son, daughter, and daughter in law being investigated and detained by the national security police. Mimi Yuen, a US citizen but Hong Kong by birth, and the eldest daughter of Elmer Yuen, was taken away by the police once she arrived Hong Kong a few days ago. It is unsure whether her US passport is being confiscated. Mimi Yuen is also a director of a listed company at the Hong Kong Stock Exchange.

Hong Kongers have been resilient when there was still genuine rule of law in the city. From the time of the colonial days to the first few years even after the 1997 handover, it was usually fun to be living in Hong Kong. In the 80s, life was quite predictable under the colonial days of Hong Kong. Fast forward to 2023 under Chinese rule. The National Security Law of Hong Kong (NSL) was enacted for more than three years now. The colonial days has been gone for 26 years since 1997. God Save the Queen no more. Primary and secondary school children of Hong Kong have to now get familiarized with the "March of the Volunteers" (義勇軍進行曲), the national anthem of the People's Republic of China. By the time this article is out, there is a strong likelihood that the Hong Kong court might have successfully banned "Glory to Hong Kong" (願榮光歸香港), the protest song of 2019 in Hong Kong, to be disseminated through the internet. It is a developing story, and my sources tell me that if the Hong Kong court ruled that "Glory to Hong Kong" is banned inside of the city, a local activist will seek judicial review (司法覆核) through the Hong Kong legal system.

People in their forties to mid-fifties belong to the Generation X category (born between 1965-1980), they are the by-products of the fruit of success of the good old Hong Kong, powered by the opening up of China in some ways. But more important, international businesses believe in the rule of law in Hong Kong, and that it would remain intact for the sake of international trade. People like my age rode on the coattail of Hong Kong's success, the city also prospered for the better in many major industries in the 80s and 90s: construction, finance, real estate and manufacturing, just to name a few. Hong Kong was on auto-pilot mode, and people with various skill sets could develop their full potential, and overseas businesses did see a lot of opportunities from just being here.

The "glory days" of Hong Kong were definitely from the 80s to about the time of the handover, and that was also a time Hong Kong people had the second wave of emigration outside of Hong Kong. They don't want to deal with the imminent change of living under Communist China, it is more of a trust factor. At every stage of life, we could be very enthusiastic and driven about work, mission and live life with a higher purpose. That said, it is difficult to be overly optimistic about Hong Kong these days.

While not trying to make direct comparison, it is sad to see the next generation of Hong Kong people, millennials (born between 1981-1996) generation Ys (born between 80s and 90s) and Zs (born between 1997-2015) alike have to confront Beijing. Activist like Joshua Wong (黃之鋒) and Agnes Chow (周庭) fit into the definition of a generation Y and Z respectively. They are raised in the days of the internet age and media, but at the same time, have taken a road less travelled to upset Beijing. We applauded Joshua and Agnes as heroes of their generation, but the communist rulers think quite differently. This is also the generation of young people that the Beijing might try to wipe out. At the time of this writing, Joshua Wong is behind bars for his political activities, and Agnes Chow has been out of jail, and remained silent ever since.

The summer months of 2019 leading to now was unprecedented in Hong Kong modern history. People across different generations came to the streets and fight for a free Hong Kong. Among those, one million came out, then two million, both during June of 2019, telling Beijing that Hong Kong people don't want to be extradited to China, and that what people want was true autonomy and democracy. During the fight for freedom in the summer months of 2019, leading to the freedom fight finale at Chinese University of Hong Kong and Polytechnic University, the younger generation have put their lives on the line for a free Hong Kong. They don't want Beijing's intrusion.

It has become quite clear that Beijing nor the puppet Hong Kong SAR government want genuine reconciliation with the Hong Kong people since the events of 2019. The level of government suppression is just unbelievable. Government injustice towards its own people will lead to more resistance and tragedy, and even death. In fact, Beijing is losing a lot of audience here. Different generations of Hong Kong people have already lost faith in the government, and if the regime only know how to respond to its people with further suppression, I believe more people will take it to the world stage level for help. If Hong Kong voices cannot be heard at the world stage, then what is left for this city? Before it is really "game over" for this city, it is the moral duty for Hong Kong people, whether situated locally or overseas, to continue to fight for our freedoms. Our voices should become one. May Glory Be to Hong Kong someday.

For Freedom: Tibet, Democratic China, and Hong Kong

I became an "accidental activist" during the Occupy Central/ Umbrella Movement of 2013-2014 in Hong Kong. Circumstances led me to step out of my comfort zone and raise my voice passionately for human rights and democracy over the past decade. It's important to clarify that I didn't attend every demonstration or protest during the time Hong Kong still allowed them. Instead, I chose to use my pen to contribute articles to local publications in Hong Kong, such as the Hong Kong Economic Journal (HKEJ), Apple Daily, and the D100 Radio internet platform, to express the city's social and political concerns.

My first encounter with self-censorship and "political interference" occurred when HKEJ terminated my weekly opinion column in early September 2014. It had run for years since 2007, just weeks before the Occupy Central movement began. The warning came from HKEJ's editor-in-chief, who advised me to focus on finance and investments, not politics. This caution came two weeks before HKEJ terminated my column contribution in the summer of 2014.

The Occupy Central movement in Hong Kong was distinct from

movements like "Occupy" in the United States, which criticized the "ruling class" and corporate greed. Hong Kong people's demands were for true autonomy under the "one country, two systems" framework. Combined with what we later called the Umbrella Movement, Hong Kong experienced 79 days of an "Occupy Event." Regrettably, Hong Kong's people never achieved their demands for a genuine election without pre-screening, as Beijing never truly desired to grant Hong Kong's people real freedom and autonomy.

For those interested in delving deeper into Hong Kong's press freedom situation, let me provide you with an update on the fate of HKEJ. Like many other local media in Hong Kong, it is now expected to align with the "Party Line" under the National Security Law (NSL). The influential founder of HKEJ, Lam Shan Muk (林山木), ceased contributing his opinion column several years ago, and it's believed that objective criticism and free speech no longer have a place in Hong Kong. Influential columnists were either told to stop writing or chose to quit due to political pressure. The deterioration of free speech in Hong Kong is evident, as reported by organizations such as Reporters Without Borders (RSF). Furthermore, several news agencies have relocated from Hong Kong to Taiwan for security reasons.

I continued to write for Apple Daily and Next Magazine, both controlled by the now-dissolved Next Digital, founded by entrepreneur Mr. Jimmy Lai. However, as many of us in Hong Kong remember, Lai's media group was forcibly shut down by the Hong Kong government in 2021, with Beijing's support. The last print copy of Apple Daily was published on June 24, 2021. The English editor in charge of Apple Daily was arrested at the airport on June 26, 2021. Among other arrests, five members of the senior management and editorial board of Apple Daily remain detained, waiting for trial as of today. Together with Jimmy Lai, the totalitarian regime plans to put the "Apple Daily Seven" on trial in the coming September.

As a contributing writer for Apple Daily, I made the tough decision to "relocate" outside of Hong Kong in June 2021, allowing me to continue writing and speaking fearlessly. Epoch Times is one platform through which I continue sharing the real Hong Kong story, and I'm delighted to be a part of it. Another platform for reaching out is my YouTube channel @EdChinWorld, designed for those who seek to understand the genuine Hong Kong situation. My current "calling" is to support the diaspora community of Hong Kong and raise a loud voice for those unjustly detained and imprisoned due to the NSL. This has become my highest purpose since leaving the city.

It's crucial not to harbor any false pretenses that Hong Kong has returned to "normal" when the most compassionate, spirited, and loving people of Hong Kong are imprisoned for their belief in freedom and democracy. We mustn't forget the sons and daughters of this city, including activists from various disciplines such as teachers, students, entrepreneurs, lawyers, social workers, legislators, and district councilors of Hong Kong. They've sacrificed their freedom, and it's our duty to support them. Their struggle is also our fight as the people of the free world; otherwise, Hong Kong will never regain its freedom if we give up.

As we approach the 34th commemoration of the June 4 Tiananmen crackdown, let me recount stories of what transpired in 1959, 1989, and 2019 in chronological order. I'll focus on the sufferings of Tibet, the tragedy of Tiananmen, and the fight of Hong Kong. This perspective is based on my recollection and research as a Hong Konger.

The Chinese Communist Party's (CCP) suppression and surveillance methods have been surreal, especially for ethnic minorities. Take, for instance, the case of the Panchen Lama, the second most important religious figure in Tibetan culture after the Dalai Lama. The 11th Panchen Lama was taken by the CCP at the age of six and has remained in China's custody for over 27 years. This young boy, if he's still alive, would be around 32 years old. Although Tibetan issues might seem distinct from Hong Kong, there are striking similarities in terms of suppression and decline.

Tibet was annexed by China, and its spiritual leader, His Holiness the 14th Dalai Lama, had to flee Tibet to escape CCP arrests in 1959. While Tibetans outside of Tibet managed to establish the Tibetan Government in Exile in India, their population was small. When the Dalai Lama fled in 1959, only around 80,000 Tibetans were able to follow. Since the "great escape of 1959," and up to the present day, the Tibetan population outside of Tibet numbers less than 100,000, which is relatively small. Nonetheless, their voices have resonated in the international community, particularly during the annual Tibetan Uprising on March 10th since 1959, a reminder to the CCP and the free world of the atrocities committed.

From a Hong Konger's perspective, my understanding of the Tibetan story is as follows: Tibetans have been in exile since 1959. At that time, around 6 million Tibetans lived inside Tibet. Of this population, 1.2 million were executed by the CCP, which constitutes a form of ethnic genocide since the occupation. The 14th Dalai Lama (born in 1935) remains an important voice for the Tibetan people and humanity. Tibetans still vividly recall how they lost their country, their religion, and the uprisings. They remember the selfless sacrifice of Tibetans through self-immolation, reminding the world that they are still fighting for their freedoms.

To the CCP, purging the memories of the Dalai Lama from Tibetans and demonizing him is part of their agenda. However, Tibetans have proven resilient and resistant to brainwashing. While some believe the 14th Dalai Lama, now 87 years old, is approaching the end of his life, the true Tibetan story will persist. The Tibetan race and their suffering will not be forgotten.

Let's fast forward 30 years and shift our focus to the Tiananmen crackdown of 1989. As we approach the 34th anniversary of the event, the political atmosphere in Hong Kong remains tense. Since the implementation of the National Security Law (NSL) nearly three years ago, the city has been silenced, much like what's happening at Tiananmen Square in Beijing. The Hong Kong Alliance in Support of Patriotic Democratic Movements of China (支聯會), which organized the Tiananmen memorial at Victoria Park in Hong Kong for over three decades, was forcibly dissolved by communist Hong Kong and the Chinese Communist Party (CCP).

The CCP has made it clear that large-scale gatherings are strictly prohibited, and communist Hong Kong's treatment of protests and public assemblies mirrors that of the rest of communist China. Those who attempted to enter Victoria Park over the past few years after 2019 have paid a steep price. The key organizers of the Hong Kong Alliance in Support of Patriotic Democratic Movements of China (支聯會) are either serving prison terms or are detained, a situation nobody could have foreseen.

It's truly tragic to witness Hong Kong's autonomy eroding rapidly and the 34th-anniversary commemoration of the Tiananmen crackdown not taking place in the city. Despite the distinctions between the people of Hong Kong and China, we now observe significant similarities between the prisoners of conscience in communist China and those in Hong Kong. The demands of Hong Kong's people go unheard, and those who resist face severe punishment, mirroring the fate of those in communist China. Both Hong Kong people and those inside communist China are united in their fight against the evil totalitarian regime.

Former paramount leader Deng Xiaoping was a controversial figure, especially in the aftermath of the Tiananmen massacre. People began to see him differently. Deng championed economic reforms to attract foreign investments, promising a legal and orderly environment that would earn the trust of the international community. He even assured, after the 1997 Handover of Hong Kong to China, that "horse racing continues, dancers still dance, and criticism of the CCP, even if it occurs, won't bring down the Party." However, fast-forwarding to 2023, it's evident that Deng's vision for maintaining Hong Kong's autonomy from the rest of communist

China has failed under the CCP's leadership. Under Xi Jinping, Hong Kong has entered another dark age, and further elaboration is unnecessary.

As each day grows darker for Hong Kong, reminiscing about the old "glory days" of our colonial past serves no purpose. We must continue to speak out strongly for Tibet, Tiananmen, and Hong Kong. There's an abundance of information available in cyberspace regarding the wrongdoings of China's communist tyranny, both in 1959, 1989, and 2019. In closing, our collective hope is that a free Tibet, a free Hong Kong, and a democratic China will become a reality someday.

Remain Steadfast in Supporting Taiwan and Hong Kong

March is a month marked by significant strategic moves from world leaders. Let's begin with a broad view of global events before delving into the perspective from Hong Kong. The highly publicized meeting between China's Xi Jinping and Russia's Vladimir Putin in Moscow has garnered immense international attention during an unprecedented period. Xi and Putin seem to believe that a major transformation is on the horizon. Concurrently, an international arrest warrant was issued for Putin by the International Criminal Court (ICC) on war crime charges related to the conflict in Ukraine. However, Russia's "Investigative Committee" contends that there are no grounds for criminal liability on Putin's part.

Around the same time, Japan's Prime Minister, Fumio Kishida, embarked on a surprising visit to Ukraine, where he met with Ukrainian President Volodymyr Zelensky. In the United States, former President Trump is facing potential indictment and arrest over alleged hush money payments to a porn star during the final days of the 2016 presidential campaign. Furthermore, there are allegations that the Chinese Communist Party (CCP) influenced and infiltrated the Canadian election in 2021.

This prompts questions like whether Xi Jinping, China's paramount leader, is contemplating an attack on Taiwan and, similar to the situation in Ukraine, whether the free world is prepared and willing to come to the defense of the island state.

The mounting geopolitical tensions between the Western world and the China-Russia alliance have introduced considerable uncertainty for Hong Kong. Foreign businesses with longstanding operations in Hong Kong are feeling the heat, with concerns about the safety of their assets. Doubts about the integrity of Hong Kong's legal system persist. Since the beginning of the Russia-Ukraine war in February 2022, superyachts belonging to Russian oligarchs with close ties to Vladimir Putin have been observed docking at Hong Kong ports. While the US, UK, and EU are working to seize the assets of Russian leaders and oligarchs worldwide in response to Russia's invasion of Ukraine, the city provides a safe haven for these various stakeholders. Hong Kong Chief Executive John Lee stated that the city would only comply with United Nations sanctions. It's worth noting that John Lee played a central role in suppressing Hong Kong's freedoms and is currently sanctioned by the United States government.

By any means necessary, China and Russia have declared the formation of a strategic alliance "with no limits." China has strengthened its trade and military ties with Russia recently. Meanwhile, China's

12-point peace plan for Ukraine and Russia has been met with skepticism. When it comes to Taiwan, is the free world prepared to confront autocratic China and, if necessary, engage in conflict to protect the island state? Xi Jinping's ambition to subdue Taiwan should not be underestimated. Hong Kong, often considered a failed model of "one country, two systems," only adds to the complexity of the situation. With Taiwan's upcoming election in January 2024, additional uncertainties are introduced into the power dynamic in the Taiwan Strait. With Xi and Putin firmly committed to maintaining their authoritarian rule, and considering Xi's aggressive stance toward Taiwan, it's essential for the United States and its democratic allies to be resolute in protecting the island state and thwarting any potential military action by communist China.

Reflecting on history, the 2014 Sunflower Student Movement in Taiwan gave rise to a new generation of activists who opposed the ruling Kuomintang (KMT) party. The KMT had attempted to hastily pass a free trade pact with China without proper review and scrutiny, and Taiwan's President at the time was Ma Ying Jeou. Ironically, as of this writing, Ma, who is no longer president, is currently on a 12-day visit to China. The Sunflower Movement, which occurred in March 2014, led to significant political change in 2016. The Democratic Progressive Party (DPP) assumed power after winning the 2016 election, replacing the

KMT. A significant portion of the Taiwanese population opposes the so-called "1992 Consensus" and the idea of "one country, two systems" for reunification with communist China. This opposition cost the KMT votes in the 2016 election, resulting in Tsai Ing Wen becoming the new president of Taiwan, a position she still holds today.

Meanwhile, in Hong Kong, the "one country, two systems" experiment has unequivocally failed since the 2019 social movement. With the National Security Law (NSL) in effect since June 2020, Hongkongers have witnessed the rapid and harsh suppression of their freedoms over the past few years. All opposition voices in the city have been silenced, and the totalitarian regime has dismantled the operations of 1) Apple Daily, 2) The Alliance (organizers of Tiananmen vigils), and 3) Democratic voices at all levels, disqualifying opposition candidates during elections, effectively changing the rules of the game in the city.

Prominent members of the Hong Kong Alliance in Support of Patriotic Democratic Movements of China, including Lee Cheuk Yan, Albert Ho, and Hang Tung Chow, have been charged with incitement to subvert state power. Additionally, the 47 activists currently on trial for participating in a primary election and the senior executives of Apple Daily and Stand News are at the center of the NSL spotlight. The Hong Kong court is busier than ever with these cases.

For a closer look at individual cases, consider former Hong Kong Alliance leader Lee Cheuk Yan. He has already been sentenced to 20 months for his involvement in three unauthorized rallies during the 2019 anti-government protests. Alongside Albert Ho and Hang Tung Chow, the trio was charged in 2021 with "inciting subversion" for their leadership in organizing the Tiananmen vigils in Hong Kong. Lee Cheuk Yan's wife, Elizabeth Tang, recently returned to Hong Kong from the UK after learning of her husband's accident inside Stanley Prison. She was subsequently arrested following her prison visit. Pro-Beijing publication Wen Wei Po (文匯報) exclusively reported her arrest. It is alleged that the NGO she headed was suspected of receiving more than $12.7 million in donations from organizations in the United States, Germany, and Norway since 1994 to support labor movements in Asia. She is currently out on bail, but her passport has been confiscated, and she cannot leave Hong Kong.

The description of Hong Kong's dismantling process and the analysis of geopolitical developments in Taiwan could continue indefinitely. However, let me conclude this piece with a philosophical reflection on the situation in Hong Kong. I left Hong Kong rather abruptly at the end of June 2021, just two days after my English editor from Apple Daily in Hong Kong was detained at the Hong Kong International Airport. Since my departure nearly two years ago, the city's DNA has undergone a dramatic transformation.

I am now more engaged in activist work outside of Hong Kong than ever before. If suppression intensifies in Hong Kong, we must redouble our efforts to support those who have been unjustly imprisoned. Perhaps I am grappling with a form of survivor's guilt, but when we think about the activists who have sacrificed and lost their freedoms, the challenges we face in advocating for Hong Kong pale in comparison. I am committed to sharing the true Hong Kong story, and we must rally support for Taiwan in its resistance against tyranny.

Erosion of Rights: Hong Kong's Dismantling Under Totalitarian Control

In less than three years following the imposition of the National Security Law (NSL), Hong Kong has undergone a dramatic transformation orchestrated by the totalitarian regimes of both communist Hong Kong and China. The once vibrant city has lost its vibrancy and dynamism. Xia Baolong, director of the Hong Kong and Macau Affairs Office, concluded his April visit to Hong Kong by delivering rhetoric borrowed from paramount leader Deng Xiaoping, offering a superficial portrayal of the suppressed Hongkongers' limited means of expression.

Within a span of four years, the spirited protests and demonstrations that once defined Hong Kong have vanished. The city's landscape no longer sees millions protesting on its streets, thanks to tightened restrictions and deceitful governance under the communist Hong Kong regime. The Labor Day demonstration scheduled for May 1 was annulled after the organizer, Joe Wong, the former chairperson of the now-defunct pro-democracy coalition, the Hong Kong Confederation of Trade Unions (HKCTU), experienced unexplained disappearances and police interrogations. Under the shadow of the NSL, freedom of peaceful assembly in Hong Kong is being stifled.

Hong Kong is experiencing a hemorrhage of capital fleeing abroad, and emigration continues unabated. The city is undergoing a metaphorical "blood transfusion" as its citizens are left disillusioned and uncertain about their future. The traditional core values of Hong Kong-freedom of speech, free press, and the liberty of demonstration-are rapidly disintegrating and being redefined. Residents, comparing life before and after the NSL, perceive the painful divergence.

In the pre-NSL era, Hong Kong welcomed diverse voices from across the political spectrum. It was a city where the rule of law was paramount, and the financial hub of the world. However, the advent of the NSL brought disillusionment and a so-called "perfecting of the electoral system," turning the Legislative Council into a house of mere "hand-raisers" where critical debates over proposed bills before their passing have become obsolete.

Quoting historic Chinese leaders like Deng Xiaoping and Mao Zedong has its irony. Presently, China's powerful elite, mostly linked with the CCP, are stashing away trillions of dollars in offshore accounts, contributing to an economic crisis. Amidst this, the real issue lies in the handling of Hong Kong citizens' retirement funds, particularly affecting those who migrated to the UK through the BNO scheme. Punishments by the Hong Kong government, through blocked access to retirement assets, are viewed as politically driven.

From a human rights standpoint, the once-held version of "one country, two systems" no longer exists. Life for political prisoners within Hong Kong's prisons or for citizens living within the city itself can be likened to a form of mental imprisonment. The struggle since the 2019 Hong Kong Extradition Bill crisis has led to an unrecognizable transformation within the city. The extreme conditions inside Hong Kong's prisons and the loss of freedoms outside them paint a grim picture of the situation.

In this transformation towards a police state, the injustice of political detentions equates to a psychological form of torture. Hong Kong's failed "one country, two systems" experiment serves as a grim reminder of what might await if Taiwan faces the aggression of the CCP.

Hongkongers Must Live as We Always Live-Global Citizens

Global tensions have reached unprecedented levels, with China's alleged "surveillance balloon program" spanning five continents grabbing international attention, setting the stage for more significant concerns. On the third Monday in February, resembling the US federal holiday of Presidents Day, President Joe Biden made an unexpected visit to the war-torn capital of Kyiv in Ukraine, holding a joint conference with President Volodymyr Zelenskyy. His message was clear: "It's not just about freedom in Ukraine; it's about freedom and democracy at large."

With unwavering support from the US and NATO for Ukraine against Russia, another pressing concern emerges: China's alleged involvement in supporting Russia with weapons against Ukraine. Could this draw our world closer to a third world war? February 24th, 2023, marked the one-year anniversary of Russia's invasion of Ukraine. People in the free world, who still have the freedom to express themselves, may need to take a stand. However, for Hongkongers, especially those residing in the city, taking a political stance is no longer easy. The extreme transformation that has occurred over the past three years since the implementation of the

National Security Law (NSL) is surreal.

If there is sufficient evidence to prove that communist China is arming Russia, the consequences will be severe. Hongkongers must stand up for what is right, harkening back to the old Hong Kong with its core values. However, Beijing stripped away their freedoms with the implementation of the NSL on June 30, 2020. The challenge now is to regain relevance when the world is witnessing the fading of the "one country, two systems" model that was once a source of pride, but now is barely believed. In a city overshadowed by a growing police state, it's challenging to stand in solidarity with Ukraine.

I recently had a one-hour political discussion with Lew Mon Hung, a former member of the National Committee of the Chinese People's Political Consultative Conference (CPPCC), on my YouTube channel, Ed Chin World. While I currently operate from abroad, Lew remains in Hong Kong. Last year, he authored an op-ed in Ming Pao, a local Hong Kong newspaper, expressing his stance on the Soviet invasion of Ukraine. He used the term "invasion" to describe it. He encountered difficulties getting a subsequent op-ed published in Ming Pao, as he claimed that the newspaper's editor offered lame excuses. It's clear that communist China and Russia maintain a close political alliance. In the current climate of Hong Kong, it's challenging for those, like Lew, who are loyal to China yet willing to offer criticism. Media censorship is widespread in Hong Kong now, and "loyalists" face intense scrutiny, making it difficult for anyone to express themselves freely. The Chinese Communist Party (CCP) is fostering an environment of fear and distrust in Hong Kong, subjecting everyone to extreme scrutiny.

Two months into the new year, 2023 promises to be a year filled with significant challenges. Hong Kong's Chief Executive, John Lee Ka Chiu, assumes the role of telling "good stories of Hong Kong." Meanwhile, Finance Secretary Paul Chan recently attended the World Economic Forum (WEF) in Davos, Switzerland, claiming that Hong Kong had returned to "normalcy." In reality, the totalitarian regime imprisoned nearly 2,000 people and arrested over 10,000 because of their efforts to fight for freedom in 2019. It's questionable whether there are any "good stories" to tell.

I returned to Hong Kong in 2000 and left the city abruptly twenty-one years later after my English editor from Apple Daily was detained at the airport in June 2021. I've witnessed numerous commentators from Hong Kong leaving the city when their freedom of speech is suppressed, and their personal freedom is at risk. On a broader scale, amid escalating geopolitical tensions and the world witnessing communist China's suppression in Hong Kong, Tibet, and Xinjiang, it's clear that "sanctions" on communist China could affect Hong Kong. The world is questioning Hong Kong's judicial independence, astounded by Chief Executive John Lee's request for Beijing's interpretation regarding whether media tycoon Jimmy Lai, the founder of Apple Daily, can hire a British lawyer to defend him in court, despite the city's Court of Final Appeal having already granted approval. At a broader level, the world is witnessing the Hong Kong government embracing authoritarian doctrines from communist China, ultimately destroying Hong Kong's autonomy.

Hongkongers have mostly employed peaceful means to convey to Beijing that the authorities should respect Hong Kong's autonomy and adhere to the original "one country, two systems" concept as outlined by Deng Xiaoping. However, this approach has failed. With the drastic electoral system changes and the ambiguity in the NSL's interpretation, Hong Kong's rule of law is gradually merging into communist China's opaque legal system. Hong Kong's DNA is irrevocably altered, and under the guise of national security, entry denials, visa cancellations, deportations, and asset freezes have become the new norm. Everyone is on high alert.

In the midst of numerous unjust NSL trials, it's evident that the law takes precedence over Hong Kong's Basic Law in protecting rights. Many who have left Hong Kong may be reluctant to return anytime soon. It's ironic to see Chief Executive John Lee spearhead a "Tell Good Stories of Hong Kong" campaign when he is among the eleven Hong Kong and mainland officials sanctioned by the US Treasury Department under the Trump administration, a sanction that remains in effect. These officials played a significant role in aiding Hong Kong's crackdown during the 2019 social movement and undermining Hong Kong's autonomy and democratic processes.

In conclusion, as Hongkongers, we must defend our city to the best of our abilities, regardless of where we are. Hongkongers and Ukrainians share the burden of defending freedoms and democracy in Asia and Europe, respectively. Ukrainians have demonstrated to the world that freedom is worth fighting for, even with their lives. Meanwhile, Hongkongers living in the city are forced into silence. As global citizens, we must unite against tyranny.

The Fall of Hong Kong Under the National Security Law

Once upon a time, Hong Kong undeniably stood as one of the world's greatest cities, known for its low tax rates, proximity to other Asian countries for weekend getaways, and high life expectancy. Above all, it was celebrated as one of the "freest cities" on the planet and a prominent international financial center in Asia. As someone who spent a substantial 20 years of my professional life working in the hedge fund industry in Hong Kong until mid-2021, I won't deny that fact. That was the era of the "old Hong Kong" when things were thriving.

However, with the National Security Law (NSL) coming into effect on June 30th, 2020, the last 2 ½ years have witnessed brutal changes in Hong Kong. This extreme political makeover has transformed the city into a gradual police state, destroying the rule of law and rendering the "one country, two systems" model a myth and a mockery. In the name of national security, the totalitarian regime, described as "factotums" in a recent opinion piece in the WSJ about media tycoon Jimmy Lai's unjust trial, has dragged the once esteemed financial city's reputation to an all-time low.

It was profoundly shocking when the Hong Kong Stock Exchange (HKEx) announced the delisting of Next Digital, the parent company of Apple Daily, founded by media tycoon Jimmy Lai and a political detainee, on January 13th, 2023. Jimmy Lai's international legal team, with a presence in the UK, recently requested a meeting with UK Prime Minister Rishi Sunak. Mr. Lai's NSL trial is scheduled for September this year. The Hong Kong government hastily issued a statement after Mr. Lai's UK lawyers and his son Sebastian Lai met with a junior minister from the UK foreign office. The statement accused Mr. Lai's international legal team of seeking to "undermine Hong Kong's rule of law and interfere with the city's judicial independence."

This accusation couldn't be further from the truth. Mr. Lai is facing multiple charges under the NSL because he is a prominent business and democracy figure who has risked his life to resist tyranny. The propaganda machinery of communist Hong Kong and communist China has relentlessly discredited him and other prominent dissidents. The only "crime" committed by Mr. Lai and others like him was writing thought-provoking pieces about the CCP's policies and advocating for the genuine return of the "one country, two systems." But we're dealing with a ruthless regime whose ultimate aim is to silence critics through fear, imprisonment, or asset confiscation. Moreover, the confiscation of passports for "investigation" by NSL police has led to arbitrary arrests and detentions within Hong Kong. This climate of detention and harassment raises concerns in the business community, particularly for those engaged in international business with and within Hong Kong.

As we enter 2023 and Chinese New Year approaches, the Hang Seng Index, which gauges the performance of the Hong Kong stock market, has rebounded from its late-October 2022 lows of 15,000 points to around 21,000 points. With China's relaxation of COVID-19 travel policies, there's a general perception that mainland visitors coming to Hong Kong will boost the economy through lavish consumer spending. It's also reported that state-owned banks in China with Hong Kong subsidiaries are enticing deep-pocketed mainland visitors to open bank deposit accounts in the city. If the deposit reaches at least HKD 4 million (US$513,000), the mainland visitor will receive a free Covid-19 mRNA Pfizer-BioNTech vaccine, which is generally unavailable in mainland China. China Citic Bank Corp, a state-owned bank, is the first to promote this incentive. Delving further into Citic Bank's promotion, mainland visitors can also enjoy a 15% discount on stays at the renowned Four Seasons Hotel and have the opportunity to test drive a luxurious Bentley. It's quite an enticing scheme to attract wealthy individuals from communist China.

In the new Hong Kong under the NSL, a high degree of autonomy no longer exists. While loyalists encourage Hongkongers to embrace the new law, the people's rights continue to erode. The city is not dead; it has transformed into something else. The "Lion Rock Spirit" that once fostered opportunities has faded, and businesses are already preparing their "Plan B" to exit and establish themselves in places like Singapore, Taiwan, and Japan, where the rule of law remains intact.

On a broader scale, communist China's paramount leader, Xi Jinping, has strained relations with neighboring countries. There is a looming geopolitical earthquake in Asia, with China taking an offensive stance, including the intention to reclaim Taiwan by force. In this scenario, Hong Kong's role remains uncertain. Will Beijing trust the people of Hong Kong enough, under the nearly defunct "one country, two systems," to consider them as "one of them"? Due to the inability to prove the allegiance of every Hongkonger, there may be further crackdowns in the city. If Taiwan is attacked, Hongkongers should carefully consider the timing and their final opportunity to leave. A doomsday scenario for Hong Kong should be on everyone's mind before it's too late.

Human Rights Situation in Hong Kong Under CCP Rule

As we approach Christmas, the atmosphere in communist Hong Kong feels increasingly stifling. These days, I wake up with a heavy heart. I had a fulfilling career in the hedge fund industry and was an active columnist in Hong Kong's finance and political arena. I also played a part in advocating for press freedom in the city. In mid-2021, I left Hong Kong involuntarily due to the prevailing political uncertainty. In a year and a half, the transformation of my beloved Hong Kong has been nothing short of surreal. The once internationally renowned city has transitioned from a semi-autonomous region to an absolute police state. In reality, it's the Hong Kong Liaison Office (中聯辦), directed by Beijing, that calls the shots.

To be precise, it has been two and a half years since the implementation of the National Security Law (NSL) in Hong Kong on June 30th, 2020, at 11:00 pm. The political landscape has undergone drastic changes. Freedom of speech, originally protected by the Hong Kong Basic Law, the city's mini constitution, is now under threat. Anything the government deems a threat can lead to arrests.

Communist Hong Kong and communist China broadly categorize numerous actions as secession, subversion, terrorism, or collusion with foreign forces. Activists from all walks of life have been detained, with over two hundred serving nearly two years in jail. My hope for the "one country two systems" (1C2S) Deng Xiaoping 1.0 model has been completely shattered by the NSL. The rule of law has been supplanted by the rule of fear.

As Christmas approaches, many people take the time for reflection. Others contemplate the future. What does the future hold for Hong Kong? At this moment, I think of the political prisoner Jimmy Lai, a media tycoon and the founder of Next Media and Apple Daily. Mr. Lai, aged 75, has been a staunch defender of press freedom and human rights. He has received numerous humanitarian and press awards. He has already been sentenced to 14 months for unauthorized assembly and a hefty 5 years and 9 months for fraud charges. However, the most critical trial is yet to come: the alleged NSL violation, with the trial continually postponed until September 2023. It is a trial without a jury, and most believe the outcome is predetermined. According to Reporters Without Borders (RSF), China and Hong Kong together have the highest number of jailed journalists, totaling 110, contributing to a global high of 533 in 2022. One last point regarding Mr. Lai is that he may spend the rest of his life in prison due to the alleged NSL charge of "colluding with a foreign power."

Since the pro-democracy newspaper Apple Daily was forced to close down in June of the previous year, the "mainstream" media in Hong Kong has largely aligned with Beijing. On the airwaves, we've witnessed the Hong Kong Government spending money to promote the "love mainland China" doctrine. The Chinese Communist Party (CCP) now fully controls the media in Hong Kong, and the city has lost its vibrancy. If you believe that the Deng Xiaoping's IC2S model still exists, you are living in a fantasy. Hongkongers have not only lost their freedom of speech and assembly but have also technically lost the right to protest.

The story doesn't end there. Even the once pro-Beijing business figures in Hong Kong are now feeling the heat of suppression. Pledging loyalty to communist China does not guarantee immunity or safety in Hong Kong. We've witnessed infighting among party members inside communist China. Political purges are common, and countless individuals with good intentions have been wrongfully persecuted. Returning to the Hong Kong front, there are speculations that super-rich tycoons in Hong Kong, particularly those with significant political influence, have been "advised" not to leave the city during specific events, such as the 20th National Congress of the Chinese Communist Party (二十大) held in October. This is to demonstrate "unity" at a time when the Chinese economy is under pressure. Most of the tycoons in Hong Kong hold foreign passports and now understand that a pro-government and pro-Beijing stance does not guarantee political or financial security. Asset freezes and passport confiscations are becoming worrisome. The elderly tycoons recall why they fled from Shanghai to Hong Kong in the 1950s when the communists took control of China's sovereignty in 1949. It's as if history is repeating itself.

I once heard a saying that goes, "Hong Kong is not just a city. It is a happening." Hong Kong's colonial history offered a unique opportunity for the city to thrive. However, since the handover in 1997, which was supposed to last for 50 years with a non-intervention policy, only 23 years have passed. Looking ahead, I anticipate that international businesses will shift their Asian headquarters from Hong Kong to other Asian cities, such as Singapore, Taipei, or Tokyo, where there is more political certainty and a stable business environment. To compound matters, the CCP has escalated its efforts and intensified its crackdown on Hong Kong, gradually reducing it to just another Chinese city. This rapid transformation is altering the very essence of Hong Kong.

Including the alleged NSL violators, there are nearly 2000 detainees in Hong Kong's prison system linked to the 2019 democracy movement. This is a significant number by any measure. The NSL is used as a political tool to criminalize Hongkongers, employing its vague and extensive definitions of secession, sedition, collusion with foreign powers, and granting absolute power and a so-called legal basis to punish dissenters. The broad and ambiguous definition of inciting seditious activities extends to re-education, beginning at an early age, even in kindergartens, with the aim of eradicating any thoughts of resistance.

In conclusion, in just two and a half years, Hong Kong has transformed itself into one of the most heavily policed and surveilled cities, comparable to Xinjiang and Tibet. We remember the death of Nobel Peace Prize laureate Liu Xiaobo, who passed away in July 2017 while in the custody of the CCP. One last point, the communist Hong Kong government and Beijing have refused to grant human rights activist and media tycoon Jimmy Lai bail - all for political reasons. Mr. Lai may indeed spend his life in prison. If this scenario unfolds, the CCP and communist Hong Kong will turn Mr. Jimmy Lai into a martyr.

Standing Unjust Trials in Hong Kong

Let's rewind to the years 2020 and 2021 in Hong Kong. The raids on Next Digital, the parent company of Apple Daily and Next Magazine in Cheung Kwan O on August 10, 2020, and June 17, 2021, involving more than 300 and 500 police officers, to suppress freedom and democracy, were beyond belief. As we all know, the "red line" of the National Security Law (NSL) has been vague and ever-shifting, creating a chilling effect for everyone. The core management team of Apple Daily has been detained for almost two years, including the CEO, associate publisher, editor-in-chief, deputy editor-in-chief, English chief editor, and political editor, all detained without bail. The founder of Next Media, Jimmy Lai, has been detained for the longest period and may face imprisonment for life.

Mr. Lai's upcoming NSL trial in December will be held in a court without a jury, with his sentence determined by three NSL judges. Moreover, there are concerns that the UK barrister representing Jimmy Lai may be prevented from representing him in the national security court by the Hong Kong government. The Hong Kong Department of Justice has appealed the court's decision to allow media tycoon Jimmy Lai to choose a defence lawyer from overseas. Article 35 of the Basic Law in Hong Kong clearly states that "Hong Kong residents shall have the right to confidential legal advice, access to the courts, choice of lawyers for timely protection of their lawful rights and interests or for representation in the courts, and to judicial remedies." The Communist Hong Kong government is vindictive and wants to avoid losing any cases, especially NSL cases. It is possible that the UK barrister may not be allowed to represent Jimmy Lai in court. (Latest development: On November 9, 2022, the Hong Kong court overruled the Department of Justice's appeal, allowing UK lawyer Tim Owen to defend Apple Daily founder Jimmy Lai in Hong Kong.)

On a broader scale, what remains in Hong Kong is "unfree speech." You either submit or face punishment, and shutting down a newspaper or online media outlet can be done efficiently. It is now evident to Hongkongers that the extreme transformation of Hong Kong affects everyone. No one is immune to tyranny. John Lee, who was the security minister for Hong Kong at the time, repeatedly conveyed the message, "Don't collude with Apple Daily's management in any form, or face dire consequences." John Lee ascended to the position of Chief Executive of Hong Kong on July 1, 2022, with Beijing's support, and is attempting to convince the international financial community that "Hong Kong is back to normal," even as the opposition camp is either incarcerated or in exile. During the highly controversial Global Financial Leaders Forum over the past week, despite local officials, from Financial Secretary Paul Chan to Executive Council Convenor Regina Ip, vigorously promoting the "Hong Kong Story," the international community remained skeptical of the political and economic situation. Hong Kong cannot be considered "open for business" when your safety and personal and business assets are at the mercy of Communist Hong Kong.

Regarding Apple Daily, let's rewind the clock 27 years ago. In the inaugural publication of Apple Daily on June 20, 1995, it was boldly proclaimed, "我們屬於香港," which translates to "Apple Daily belongs to Hong Kong." It was the city's only pro-democracy newspaper, and time was running out as the former British colony approached its reversion to Communist China. Apple Daily had become the most successful pro-democracy newspaper in the city. Since the implementation of the NSL, Hong Kong has become unrecognisable, with numerous forces at play attempting to suppress various freedoms. The NSL has become an illogical and formidable weapon, making a mockery of the original "one country two systems" 1.0 version. How can Hong Kongers continue with life as usual when pro-establishment figures argue that journalistic work can proceed as long as it is "lawful"? In practice, reporting news in Hong Kong puts you under scrutiny at every moment. The Foreign Correspondence Club of Hong Kong (FCC), which has long been a hub for news in Asia, is in jeopardy. Its lease expires on January 1, 2023, and the lack of indication from the Hong Kong Government Property Agency, responsible for the FCC lease, regarding the renewal of rental terms for the next five years remains uncertain.

As for the case of Next Media and Apple Daily, if the British barrister's entry to Hong Kong is revoked due to the Hong Kong Department of Justice's intervention, it would send a chilling effect to anyone considering doing business in Hong Kong. No one would be able to defend Jimmy Lai of Apple Daily. Mr. Lai's lawyers in the UK have also received death threats, such as receiving razor blades in the mail. Perhaps the Hong Kong court might assign Mr. Lai any lawyer for show and quickly pass an unjust verdict? When defending free speech and press freedom involves detaining or imprisoning the management, senior editorial staff, and the majority shareholder of the most widely read newspaper (both in print and online) in the city, the stark reality is that, under the "new normal," certain forms of journalistic reporting are no longer tolerated in Hong Kong. In a broader context, the totalitarian regime holds overarching power to decide what is legal or not, and with this broad power, one's freedoms are constrained.

International businesses operating in Hong Kong will undoubtedly question whether it is worthwhile to continue when the authorities have the power to detain and seize assets. Hong Kong appears to have uncontrolled risks within itself. Regarding Chief Executive John Lee, a former career policeman and a loyalist to Communist China in many aspects, he is certainly empowered to freeze the assets of anyone in Hong Kong and more. We have also witnessed how Hong Kong government officials adopt a "wolf warrior" mentality to counter any form of criticism. In conclusion, Hong Kong cannot be considered back to normal as long as there are political prisoners and people and money continue to leave. Over the past two years, those who remain in Hong Kong have adjusted to the "new normal" and to self-censorship to avoid so-called "troubles." They have little choice when living in fear. For Hong Kongers, wherever they are, it is essential to keep monitoring the developments of NSL trials. Hashtags like #FreeJimmyLai and #FreeHongKong are not enough; it is crucial to continue the fight, no matter where they are, to condemn and resist unjust laws and unjust trials.

Leaving Hong Kong but Continuing to Tell the Story

In October, I embarked on an intensive journey across the United States and Canada, dedicated to promoting the global release of "The Hong Konger - Jimmy Lai's Extraordinary Struggle For Freedom." I found myself in lesser-known college towns, such as Benedictine College in Kansas and Hillsdale College in Michigan, where I organised screenings and discussions about the documentary. These smaller liberal arts colleges in the U.S. displayed a strong interest in understanding the situation in Hong Kong. Despite three years passing since the anti-extradition bill protests, the world's memory of Hong Kong and its people's unwavering determination to fight for freedom and their paths to exile remains vivid. Among those exiles is Jimmy Lai, the Hong Kong media tycoon. In my travels, I also connected with Hong Kong groups that have resettled in various North American cities to share "The Hong Konger" with them.

Today's article is less about Jimmy Lai, a figure widely known for his lifelong commitment to freedom.

Instead, I want to narrate the story of an ordinary individual, a young trader with roots in Hong Kong, and how he achieved success in the city before choosing a path of exile. During my journey through North America, in a mid-sized Canadian city, I had the pleasure of meeting a young investment trader in his mid-30s. He had returned to Canada from Hong Kong due to the challenges posed by COVID-19 and political uncertainties. More than a year ago, he made the decision to leave Hong Kong after witnessing the city's decline following the enactment of the National Security Law (NSL). Our conversation unfolded in a Hong Kong-style café that served the renowned "Hong Kong milk tea."

Let's refer to my young friend as Joe. He is of Chinese ethnicity, and his parents had moved from Hong Kong to Canada a few years before the Tiananmen crackdown in 1989. Although Joe was quite young during the Tiananmen tragedy, he learned more about it as he grew into his teenage years. Joe's journey has passed swiftly. About ten years ago, he relocated to Hong Kong after graduating from a university when job opportunities were scarce. He bought a one-way ticket to Hong Kong, began as a head-hunting research assistant at a well-known recruitment agency specialising in the finance sector, and eventually entered the finance industry himself.

Joe held a bachelor's degree in finance from a major Canadian university. In summary, he climbed the ranks to become an associate portfolio manager responsible for a significant portfolio at a medium-sized asset management firm (with nearly USD 1 billion in assets under management). His salary and bonuses were substantial, averaging over USD 400,000 in total compensation per year over the last five years. Being single and having made a wise investment in a residential apartment in Hong Kong around seven years ago, Joe's net worth had also grown significantly. He sold his apartment over a year ago, realising a handsome profit before Hong Kong's real estate market took a downturn.

Over the course of ten years, Joe experienced life in Hong Kong, witnessing its ups and downs. With his substantial compensation, he managed to accumulate a net worth exceeding USD 2 million. Due to COVID-19 and the NSL, he decided to leave his job at the boutique asset management firm I mentioned earlier and resettled in the mid-sized Canadian city. Joe was always fascinated by the story and adventures of Jim Rogers, the legendary trader who once worked for hedge fund titan George Soros. Jim Rogers left Soros Fund Management as a junior partner before the age of 39, retired from fund management, and embarked on a journey around the world on a motorcycle. Joe aspires to follow in Jim Rogers' footsteps and explore the world in his own way.

In this mid-sized Canadian city, Joe contemplates using one-fifth of his net worth, approximately USD 400,000 (with a conversion rate of USD 1 to approximately 1.37 CAD), to purchase property in one of the suburbs where he used to live. He plans to invest another USD 600,000 in income-generating properties and consider placing the remaining USD 1 million in term deposits. With current rising interest rates and the stock market experiencing significant declines, Joe values cash as king. He is in no hurry to seek employment, and his priority is to explore the world and gain perspective.

Joe and I continued our conversation for hours in this Hong Kong-style café in the mid-sized Canadian city. He vividly recalled the Umbrella Movement of 2014. Although he was still relatively young in his late twenties at the time of the movement, he empathised with the student leaders in Hong Kong and understood their struggle. Whenever possible, he would even buy lunch for the students who supported the democratic movement of Hong Kong during their lunch hours. The peaceful social movement lasted for 79 days. In 2019, the fight against the Chinese Communist Party (CCP)'s intervention and "annexation" of Hong Kong was cross-generational. Joe remained "super active" in the city's social causes, such as "Fight For Freedom, Stand With Hong Kong." This put him in a "marginal case" of getting arrested due to his "front-line" activism, which was unconventional in the finance world.

Joe comprehends the demands of Hong Kongers: democracy and freedom, which are universal values across all nations. He recognises that many Hong Kongers have lost hope in the city, and Beijing's unfulfilled promises have pushed Hong Kong into a downward spiral. He realistically sees that Hong Kongers have lost hope, and, regrettably, the entire city has entered a dark era of political persecution. The core values of Hong Kong, including freedom of speech, freedom of the press, freedom of political thought, and an independent judiciary, have vanished in just two short years.

Over a year ago, Joe concluded that this was the end of Hong Kong as he knew it. For outsiders who have called Hong Kong home over the years, the disappearance of the city's dynamic spirit, the erosion of freedoms and democracy in a global financial hub, and the potential seizure of personal assets, arbitrary detention, venue closures, bank account freezes, have all diminished the once-celebrated city's status as a place to live and do business. The city's decline is surreal, with many talents migrating to neighbouring countries such as Japan and Singapore.

What the future holds for Hong Kong remains uncertain, but many have made sacrifices to defend what Hong Kong once stood for: freedom, democracy, and rights. They have endured persecution, suppression, or imprisonment. As for my friend Joe, who has experienced and benefited from Hong Kong and still considers himself an outsider but has a deep understanding of the city, I hope he remembers the better aspects of Hong Kong, such as its breathtaking mountains for hiking, its culture, history, dynamics, and efficiency.

On a more serious note, I hope Joe remembers that Hong Kongers have been selfless and fearless in defending their freedoms and rights, whether they are still in Hong Kong or "in exile" overseas. Joe has pledged to tell the Hong Kong story, capturing both its positive and negative aspects, wherever his journey takes him.

Misplaced Hope for Hong Kong's Future

As this article makes its debut, we find ourselves in the last quarter of the year, with less than 100 days remaining before 2022 draws to a close. In this piece, I aim to recap recent developments in Hong Kong that have captured the attention of people. The Hong Kong government has just announced the relaxation of quarantine restrictions for travellers entering the city, effective September 26th. Under the so-called 0+3 arrangement, international inbound travellers can now enter the city without the need for quarantine hotel stays. However, passengers on flights to Hong Kong will be required to undergo a Rapid Antigen Test (RAT) 24 hours before boarding. Upon arrival at Hong Kong airport, passengers will still need to undergo a polymerase chain reaction (PCR) test before proceeding to their homes or hotels. The first day of arrival is counted as Day 0. Travellers will also be required to take daily RAT tests for seven consecutive days, along with PCR tests on days 2, 4, and 6, resulting in a total of 11 tests up to Day 7, a truly surreal requirement.

Two significant issues have gripped Hong Kong over the past three years: the implementation of the National Security Law (NSL) and stringent COVID-19 pandemic policies. The NSL has effectively quashed civil society in Hong Kong, rendering the city more repressive. In the name of combating COVID-19, further restrictions have been imposed on Hong Kongers, curbing their freedom of movement. Incidents of police abuse have become commonplace, and individuals from the pan-democratic camp are either incarcerated or in exile. The formation of independent human rights and political groups has become nearly non-existent.

The global stage is marked by tension. Vladimir Putin of Russia has issued warnings about the potential use of nuclear weapons to "protect" his country's sovereignty while clamping down on civilians who protest in Moscow or St. Petersburg. President Xi Jinping's statements in "support" of Russia in the context of Ukraine have been meticulously worded. All eyes are on Xi's confirmation for his third term as the party chief during the 20th National Congress in mid-October.

For nearly two weeks, thousands of Hong Kongers paid their respects to the late Queen Elizabeth II of England at the British Consulate-General in Hong Kong. The consulate complex, located at 1 Supreme Court Road, Admiralty, Hong Kong Island, which intersects with Justice Drive, is one of the largest British consulates-general globally and surpasses many British embassies and high commissions. It plays a crucial role in maintaining British relations with Hong Kong and Macau.

On the evening of September 19, 2022, Hong Kong was seven hours ahead of London. While it was a regular workday in the former British colony, it was a day of national mourning for the late Queen Elizabeth II. Her state funeral ceremony was underway, viewed by billions worldwide. People in the UK and around the world tuned in to the Queen's funeral ceremony through a myriad of media networks. At the British Consulate-General in Hong Kong, in addition to laying flowers and leaving personal notes to pay their respects to the Queen, those who came to the consulate felt a sense of "belongingness" as they mourned her passing.

In the consulate's compound area, a middle-aged Hong Konger played the harmonica, performing tunes of the English national anthem "God Save The Queen" and "Glory to Hong Kong," which is regarded as the city's unofficial national anthem. The large crowd that had gathered to pay their respects to the Queen joined in and sang "Glory to Hong Kong" in Cantonese. The harmonica player, later identified by Hong Kong police as Mr. Pang, was detained within a cordoned-off area and charged with suspicion of acting with seditious intent.

Large gatherings have become a rarity in Hong Kong since the enactment of the National Security Law in mid-2020. The substantial turnout at the Queen's vigil in Hong Kong can be seen as a form of silent protest against the Chinese Communist Party (CCP). China seeks to rewrite Hong Kong's history entirely, with the authorities currently denying the existence of the 150+ years of colonial rule.

With the "evil tool" of the NSL in effect for over two years now, the deterioration of human rights in this once internationally renowned city is beyond imagination. Pragmatic Hong Kongers have accelerated their emigration plans, driven by concerns that the new Hong Kong Chief Executive John Lee Ka Chiu's administration may be more oppressive than that of his predecessor, Carrie Lam.

Those who are incarcerated, such as media tycoon Jimmy Lai, young activist Joshua Wong, or legal scholar Benny Tai, will face trial under the NSL without a jury, whether they plead guilty or not. While the West is acutely aware of the torture and ethnic genocide in Xinjiang, China, the cultural genocide in Hong Kong and the reshaping of the city's identity through brute force is nothing short of surreal.

If Beijing is wise, it should consider releasing Jimmy Lai and granting amnesty to all NSL detainees. The Chief Executive of Hong Kong possesses the authority to offer amnesty. However, the reality is that this decision does not rest with John Lee Ka Chiu. Hong Kong cannot truly be Hong Kong without genuine reconciliation with its people. In the past, Hong Kong boasted a free society, an independent judiciary, and an open media. Suppression is not the solution, and the ongoing political purge in

Hong Kong is a testament to the fact that "one country, two systems" has vanished.

The citywide crackdown continues to expand. I foresee increased turmoil in Hong Kong in the days, weeks, months, and years ahead. Let us do our best to stand with Hong Kong. The hope misplaced in Hong Kong's future is indeed disheartening. A "Free Hong Kong" remains a distant aspiration.

Hong Kong in Accelerated Exodus Mode

An analyst from Hong Kong just sent me a visual image and message. It is a front cover picture, depicting Xi Jinping in a Chinese emperor gown from a few years back. It was actually the front cover portrait of the Economist magazine. The reason why this analyst sent this satirical picture to me, has to do with the 20th CPC National Congress in China which takes place in mid-October, and whether Xi, as the current leader of China, can rule the most populated country on earth for the third term- or "forever". This hard working analyst once told me, if Xi remains in power for the third term, a lot of people in Hong Kong and China will have to take more "immediate decisions"- staying and live under fear, or leaving for the love of freedom.

Just rewind the clock back to 2020, and exactly two months before the enactment of the National Security Law (NSL) in Hong Kong. The propaganda ads put up by the government suggested that the NSL would strengthen one country, two systems in Hong Kong. The former Chief Executive (CE) of Hong Kong Carrie Lam also claimed that the NSL would affect very few people in Hong Kong. Not sure how many people would still believe that now. And just a few days ago, the former CE was caught in the social media that she went shopping in the "wet market" in Wan Chai. But this time, Lam is no longer in power, and being replaced by the no nonsense and former career police John Lee Ka Chiu.

For Hong Kong, the financial services and business sectors have "contingency plans" for the inevitable exodus, due to the once famed international city's uncertain political future. As for Hong Kong's financial services regulator, the Securities and Futures Commission (SFC) CEO Ashely Alder will step down in September. No successor is being announced, and all eyes is on this particular person. All we know is, long time deputy CEO Julia Leung will "deputize" the soon empty role of SFC head, until Beijing call the shots to find a permanent replacement. It is to the international community and industry's expectation that the SFC "should not be politicized", nor the regulator being unduly influenced by Beijing. I wish this would be the case for Hong Kong.

For businesses, as long as Hong Kong got a lot of arbitrary arrests and detainees due to the alleged violation of the National Security Law (NSL), the city will never go back to normalcy and people will stop pumping money back into the Hong Kong system. We also witnessed recently that the "selling of the Hong Kong dollars" vs the US has been at record high, and to a certain extent, it is a confidence of people's view on the confidence and stability towards the once famed international city's political and economic future. The "selling pressure" from the real estate market is also obvious, most aggressive buyers can get good bargain now, betting on Hong Kong will "recover" from all forms of turmoil. I wish the "willing sellers" will also make intelligent currency hedge, and plan for the future.

The chilling effect of the NSL has been surreal over the past two months. The NSL's definition of secession, sedition, subversion and collusion with foreign forces have been vague, but it surely has empowered the police to arrest anyone, with uncontrolled risks of abusing their power, end of story. An uplifting story developed in August though: former legislator and long time human rights activist and lawyer Albert Ho Chun Yan was allowed to go on bail, after being charged with NSL violation on "illegal assembly". He was already detained behind bars for 15 months.

The high- profile arrest on Next Media founder Jimmy Lai and its top executives more than a year ago has not been forgotten: it raised the red flag for those wanting to do business in Hong Kong. Like so many NSL detainees, almost all 200+ of them have been behind bars for more than a year, and a few close to two years before the trial begins. The unjustified act of "punishing the wrong side" did not go unnoticed, and the international community cannot be fooled twice, that Hong Kong is "back to normal". It would also be interesting to see whether the so-called "international banking forum" in Hong Kong this coming November will attract any big corporations, when Hong Kong still have restrictive COVID policy and travelling to Hong Kong is viewed by the western world as "high risks".

And back to the core of the problem: one country two systems in Hong Kong is gone. The NSL was also brought in to Hong Kong without consultation in mid 2020- it has changed the hard reality of doing businesses in Hong Kong forever. The rule of law in Hong Hong is overlayed with rule by fear. The tactics used to suppress the vocal ones in mainland China (too long a list) is now fully integrated into Hong Kong. Is there still time to come to our own rescue?

More single-family offices that I know, with names to be disguised, keep on "divesting" their Hong Kong real estate portfolios with a deep "hair cut". The owner/ portfolio manager of the family offices wants to complete all the closings sanctions as soon as possible. Offshore accounts set up in Singapore, UK, and Jersey Channel Islands to secure the sale proceeds from real estate is almost a norm for sophisticated investors. Family offices re-allocate outside of Hong Kong become a norm.

There are many other reasons for people who are residents or permanent residents of Hong Kong to resettle in other parts of the world, perhaps even temporarily. For corporates, there is no strategic advantage for global businesses to invest heavily into Hong Kong now due to political uncertainty. The exodus of funds and talents, especially from a professional level, has been a kneejerk reaction of the political unrest of Hong Kong that has changed the way of doing business in this city forever. Our Hong Kong, once an international city that most people have aspired to, has fallen from its glory. Beijing might never understand the damage has been unrepairable. For those who decide to stay, it means so much more than ever before, and good luck.

Remembrance of Apple Daily

June 20th, 1995, marked the inaugural print edition of Apple Daily in Hong Kong. Fast forward to June 24th, 2021, and we witnessed the final print run of this iconic newspaper. The raid on Next Digital, the parent company of Apple Daily and Next Magazine in Cheung Kwan O, involving 500 police officers in June of the previous year, was nothing short of surreal. It ultimately led to the newspaper's closure, and on that fateful June 24th, 2021, one million copies rolled off the printing press.

A year has passed since the closure of this pro-democracy newspaper in Hong Kong, and in its wake, online newspapers StandNews and Citizen News were also forced to shut down under political pressure. The most recent victim is FactWire, an investigative reporting agency, which ceased its operations on June 10th, 2022. The "red line" of the National Security Law (NSL) has proven to be vague and ever-shifting, creating a chilling effect that requires no explanation. For both Hong Kong residents and overseas Hong Kongers, what remains in the city today is a version of "unfree speech," where you either submit or face punishment, including "dire consequences." This reality is now all too clear for Hong Kong.

The incoming Chief Executive of Hong Kong, John Lee Ka-chiu, who is set to take office on July 1st, has previously been sanctioned by the U.S. government during the Trump administration for his role in undermining Hong Kong's autonomy. The enactment of the NSL two years ago had already created significant apprehension among the people of Hong Kong. Some may remember John Lee, who, during the "final days" of Apple Daily, was the Security Minister for Hong Kong and repeatedly appeared on television with a chilling message: "Don't collude with Apple Daily's management in any form, or else you will face dire consequences." This cast a shadow of concern over the fee-paying subscribers of Apple Daily.

Reflecting on the events one year ago, before the newspaper's closure, it would have been considered insane to think that buying or subscribing to Apple Daily could lead to official retribution in a normal society. However, Hong Kong has regrettably transformed into a society governed by fear. Back then, people hoped that the "horror show" was a temporary ordeal. Now, one year later, the "horror show" continues.

The first publication of Apple Daily on June 20th, 1995, included the line, "Apple Daily belongs to Hong Kong," emphasising that it was a newspaper for the people of Hong Kong, filling a gap in the market at the time, just two years before Hong Kong's handover from British to Chinese rule. Fast forward to 2022, one year after Apple Daily's closure, and we see that Hong Kong has become unrecognisable. Various forces are actively working to suppress the few remaining online news outlets. While I refrain from naming them, it's not difficult to discern their identities.

On the final day of Apple Daily's print edition, Thursday, June 24th, 2021, I visited my favourite newsstand in Central, Hong Kong, to obtain the last print copies of the newspaper. Many copies were needed, as I will explain in a forthcoming opinion piece in Epoch Times. I conducted a livestream on my YouTube channel: Ed Chin World, to witness this historic moment alongside journalist Sarah Liang from Epoch Times. Numerous people queued up to obtain the last issue. Some customers purchased multiple copies, possibly as an act of solidarity to support the newspaper.

One may wonder how law-abiding Hong Kong residents could continue to endure a situation where their basic right to choose what to read was not guaranteed. One year after the newspaper's closure, the answer is clear. The newspaper was silenced by brute force, orchestrated by the totalitarian regime of Communist Hong Kong and Communist China. The National Security Law has become an illogical and far-reaching weapon, making a mockery of the original "one country, two systems" principle enshrined in the Basic Law. As we approach the 25th anniversary of the so-called "one country, two systems," most people today doubt that the "two systems" still exist in Hong Kong. It seems to be nothing more than words on paper.

The word "surreal" is the only fitting description for the events that transpired when 500 police officers raided the Next Digital building last June. If defending free speech and press freedom results in putting the management, senior editorial staff, and 72 percent majority shareholder Jimmy Lai out of business or in jail, then the conclusion is simple: under the "new normal," "free press" is no longer tolerated in Hong Kong. The totalitarian regime holds overwhelming power to decide what is legal, resulting in severe restrictions. International businesses operating in Hong Kong will now question whether it's worth continuing when the authorities have the power to detain and seize. The then Security Minister John Lee was certainly empowered to freeze the assets of anyone in Hong Kong and more. Yet, he played a leading role in the "horror show" that led to Apple Daily's demise.

As the saying goes, you may chain someone's physical body, but you cannot chain their soul and spirit. Hong Kong has reached a point of no return. While we've weathered many storms in the past, a city without a major pro-democracy newspaper and with seven of Apple Daily's staff in jail due to alleged National Security Law violations signals that the political purge is far from over. The "cleansing process" by the totalitarian regime has not yet concluded.

Communist China once pledged freedom for Hong Kong-freedom of speech, freedom of the press, freedom of assembly, freedom of religion, and freedom to travel. Unfortunately, all these freedoms have been on a steady decline. In reality, true freedom no longer exists in Hong Kong. Nonetheless, we must keep the spirit of freedom alive and continue to fight for it, wherever we are. Let us not forget the seven Apple Daily employees who are now incarcerated, and the many courageous Apple Daily journalists and columnists who continued to edit, comment, and report on Hong Kong stories until the very end, in defense of our freedoms.

Jimmy Lai: Bravest Guardian of Hong Kong's Freedom in the Face of an Unjust NSL Trial

In 1991, I first met Jimmy Lai, just a year after he unveiled Next Magazine. Back then, I held the position of the Chinese head at CHIN Radio / TV International in Toronto, Canada, focusing on Hong Kong matters leading up to the 1997 handover. Our program content delved into various themes, such as immigration, resettlement, entrepreneurship, and investment strategies, resonating with migrating Hong Kongers globally. Even under British colonial rule, the latest issues of Next Magazine from Hong Kong were eagerly sought after, reaching Chinatowns across major cities worldwide a week after hitting the stands.

Since that initial meeting, I made it a priority to stay connected with Jimmy. His compelling narratives on the significance of information freedom and democracy had already sounded the alarm for Hong Kongers and the global audience, suggesting that substantial changes could unfold after the handover of Hong Kong. This was a time preceding the internet's transformative impact on communication in the mid-'90s. Subsequently, Jimmy ventured into launching Apple Daily in 1995, establishing it as the most widely read newspaper in Hong Kong, both in print and online. However, the authorities in communist-controlled Hong Kong and Beijing didn't appreciate the paper; there were raids into the paper's headquarters, leading to the arrest of six senior executives besides Jimmy. The final print and online run of the paper came to an end on June 24th, 2021.

In the mid-'90s, I shifted my focus back to the financial industry, assuming the position of a portfolio manager specializing in absolute return strategies in Canada. This move occurred before my return to Hong Kong in 2000 — three years following the handover from Great Britain to China. Despite my professional trajectory leaning towards hedge funds and asset management, my commitment to media endured. Concurrently, I resumed writing for the Hong Kong Economic Journal in 2006 and reestablished connections with Next Media. My contributions extended to the finance and political sections at Apple Daily and Next Magazine. By 2014, the Occupy Movement marked a significant phase of heightened involvement for me, evolving my role into that of a columnist and commentator. Beyond the constant pursuit of "chasing alpha" in the financial markets, I found myself passionately advocating for democracy and freedoms in response to Beijing's escalating control over Hong Kong during the social movements of 2014 and 2019.

However, the pivotal moment arrived with the unjust imposition of the National Security Law (NSL) in 2020, often compared to a "neutron bomb" detonated in Hong Kong — a massacre on our freedoms. The realization dawned that Hong Kong was on the verge of silencing all voices, and the authentic story needed to be told. Departing from Hong Kong at the end of June 2021, just four days after the forced closure of Apple Daily's final print and online versions, posed a mental and emotional challenge. Nevertheless, the English editor-in-chief at Apple Daily faced arrest at the Hong Kong airport merely two days after the newspaper's shutdown. The NSL police department engaged in a form of "random fire," attempting to arrest individuals swiftly and subjecting them to long-term detainment while confiscating their travel documents. Such occurrences were unprecedented in the "old Hong Kong."

On this Christmas Eve in Toronto, Canada, I find myself concluding this article with a philosophical touch — a moment deeply immersed in introspection. The prevailing shock lingers as notable figures in Hong Kong's recent history either endure imprisonment or are forced into exile.

Reverend Chu Yiu Ming, one of Occupy Central's trio leaders, recently graced my YouTube Channel as a special guest. Together, we immersed ourselves in the ongoing unjust National Security trial of Jimmy Lai, which commenced just a few days ago on December 18th, 2023. The trial is expected to unfold over at least 80 court days. On air, we passionately beseeched for miracles for Jimmy and others who find themselves unjustly detained, undergoing unfair trials, and awaiting their sentences. Our interactive dialogue also delved into Reverend Chu's recently released memoir, shedding light on the democracy movement in Hong Kong.

Leading up to the enactment of the National Security Law (NSL) in mid-2020, Jimmy, a devout Catholic and avid reader, found himself in a tense predicament in Hong Kong. Recognizing his need for inspiration, I recalled an autographed book I had received from His Holiness the 14th Dalai Lama, which had been sitting on the shelf for a while. It struck me that I should pass it on to Jimmy. The book, titled "My Land & My People," the autobiography of His Holiness the Dalai Lama, arrived at a crucial juncture when the totalitarian regime sought to shut down Jimmy's media group. Reflecting on an interview with His Holiness the Dalai Lama in Brussels, Belgium, a few years earlier, where he imparted the words, "Never give up hope for Hong Kong," my intention was to provide

Jimmy with a source of encouragement. This was especially significant for someone who stands as the strongest defender of Hong Kong under the "One Country Two Systems" framework. Unfortunately, the totalitarian regime failed to honor the promise and instead revoked it all after 22 years of what was supposed to be a 50-year non-intervention policy.

During this Christmas season, as I contemplate the profound meanings of life — salvation, persecution, suffering, and the highest purpose of humanity — I am deeply moved by the plight of Jimmy Lai and countless others who have fearlessly spoken out for Hong Kong, only to find themselves imprisoned due to their unwavering love for the city. Jimmy's decision to remain in Hong Kong, rooted in his faith and unwavering defense of the Christian faith, reveals a man who has steadfastly lived out his principles for over three decades.

There was a time when freedom thrived in Hong Kong, both before and after the 1997 handover, and for this, we owe a profound debt of gratitude to Jimmy. The influx of foreign capital into Hong Kong won't resume until investors are confident that the rule of law remains intact, the legal system stays impartial, and, above all, political prisoners are set free. Jimmy Lai's unjust trial in Hong Kong is poised to be closely monitored by the entire world.

As we celebrate Christmas, let's not only reflect on the joy of the season but also join in solidarity, praying for the release of Jimmy Lai and all those unjustly detained political prisoners, and nurturing hope for a Hong Kong that regains its rightful place as a bastion of freedom. Jimmy Lai's unjust NSL trial will resume on January 2nd, 2024. Let's keep paying attention to the developments.

對沖人生路 自由價更高

錢志健——著

標普納指　高位徘徊

國安惡法　香港沉淪

一國兩制　實驗幻滅

自由台灣　不容有失

反送中後　港人換血

價值之戰　時代革命

好評推薦

來自金融界的資深對沖基金經理錢志健先生，同為《港區國安法》下決定離開香港的港人之一。過往在港出版的書籍被視為「禁書」，是次在海外首次出版，暢所欲言地講述現今投資與國際關係、普世價值的關係。

國際關係學者　沈旭暉

序

錢兄的書能夠發人心醒，不能不讀，更能夠幫助讀者管理好自己的投資、富和人生。轉瞬間，已替錢兄寫了三次推介，上次寫推介的時候是二〇一九年中，在他的書《致富活著 III》中指出，鴉片戰爭背後的真正原因是國家安全，而致勝關口是「自由」，多自由就多人才，少自由就少自由，沒自由就沒人才，故此投資要找自由多、人才多的地方，相信如果二〇一九年投資美國股市，四年後的今天一定回報豐厚。

今次錢兄這本書為我們帶來甚麼思考？鴉片戰爭在一八三九年開打，到了一百八十年後的二〇一九年，國家安全仍然是頭號大事，任何一個國家都重視國家安全，只是遇見問題時是否對症下藥，是否開對藥方。大清帝國當年開錯了方，令大清帝國吃錯了藥，從此一蹶不振，病入膏肓。今天面對香港的問題又是否開對藥方？是否藥力過分猛峻？是否虛虛實實？香港是否

「香港交易所」前人力資源總監

曾振超

已上吐下瀉？錢兄的書或者在這方面提供了可能的症狀及服藥後的情況。

在今次這本書上，有一篇很有趣的文章〈香港有燶味，這個夏天螞蟻搬家〉。城市衰落，國家凋亡，這種大火災不會是突然而至，總是有燶味的，如果及時用對的救火方法可以避免大災難。上帝給耶路撒冷的神奇數字是七，所以有七十個七的精確預言。上帝給北京的神奇數字是什麼？可能是十九。每十九年華人的農曆生日就和公曆生日重疊。在北京歷史上，十九年又是多麼神奇。在《明太宗實錄・卷一七九》中記載，明朝永樂十四年（一四一六年）八月，明成祖正式在北京西宮視朝聽政，北京政權正式開始，直到一六四四年大明帝國滅亡，共兩百二十八年，即十二個十九年。外族女真族滿州人入主北京，至一九一一年大清帝國才覆亡，共兩百六十六年，即十四個十九年。中華民國正式成立也定都北京，但一九四九年又失去了在中國大陸的政權，共三十八年，即兩個十九年。中華人民共和國一九四九年成立，到二○二五年就是四個十九年，又是一個大關，如果闖得過去，或許可以有十多個十九年，可能真的東升西降，但願上主保佑中國，記念中國人民。錢兄書中所聞的燶味是真實，但會否成為大火災，要視乎未來兩年人們是否用對的方法救火或天降大雨。

至於是否需要搬家？人人不同。有財經演員指明年（二○二四）恆指升至四萬點。這個是有可能的，看阿根廷股市，二○一三年才三千多點，二○一九年就已三萬點，二○二三年更突

破十萬點。原因是什麼？阿根廷披索（ARS）大幅貶值，阿根廷在一九九一年就把披索掛鈎美元，一美元兌一披索，直到二○○三年脫鈎時立即貶了三倍，至一美元兌三披索，跟著慢慢的貶至二○一二年的四倍，今天卻已是八百倍，即一美元兌八百阿根廷披索。只要港元不跟美元掛鈎，到了這個四十多年的貨幣遊戲（currency game）也玩完的時候，按現在的M2供應，如果港元自由兌換，港元應在短期內貶四至八倍，即三十至六十港元兌一美元，那時恆指十萬點不是夢。君子和而不同，或許你的看法跟錢兄不同，但不能不看他的書，最好能及時收看他的影片，至少為自己的財富和投資做合適的對沖，以免在大時代的洪水中變得一貧如洗，如同阿根廷的人民一樣。但我依然相信，「洪水泛濫之時，耶和華坐著為王；耶和華坐著為王，直到永遠。耶和華必賜力量給他的百姓，耶和華必賜平安的福給他的百姓。」（詩篇29：10-11）

自序

筆者過去十多年間，在香港出版了十本政治加投資元素的書籍。直至二〇一九年香港反修例事件、二〇二〇年「港版國安法」實施後，因香港的政治巨變，再沒有可能出版「我手寫我心」的書了。香港的「一國兩制」，在中共不守承諾的情況下，五十年不變，近乎已全部成為了廢話。筆者在二〇一九年七月，最後的香港著作是《致富活著三》，而三本著作，即《致富活著1、2、3》，居然在香港圖書館成了「禁書」。在「愛國者治港」的年代，香港出現了「倒退一百五十年」的現象；曾經的英國殖民地給予香港的優良基石，現在卻是一一擦掉。

二〇二四年是巨變之年。有幸和新的臺灣出版社合作，延續文字精神；而文字的力量，就是希望把歷史得以承傳。寶島的自由得來不易，而在大部份香港人的眼裡，臺灣早已是「主權國家」：有自由、法治、投票權以及公民權利。而中共建議對臺灣採取的「一國兩制」，其實凶險萬分。臺海維持現狀，是最好的方法。

美國三大指數：道瓊、納斯達克、標普500指數，在整個二〇二三年，走勢依舊強勁，也極為波動。股市大行情永遠如是非，而科技股走勢則過關斬將，一步一驚心。微軟

（MSFT）、亞馬遜（AMZN）、蘋果（AAPL）及谷歌（GOOG）早已破萬億美元市值，而Nvidia（NVDA）在二〇二三年六月，也成功成為萬億美元市值的公司，創辦人黃仁勳本身是美籍的臺灣人。

本書《對沖人生路　自由價更高》，希望帶領讀者前往另一個想像空間：不單只著重投資回報，更要關注世界的事情，畢竟還有一種更重要的是「人生回報」。在我們這部新書中，會穿梭時空，但主要內容將從四年前說起，即二〇一九年。回顧二〇一九年的當時，正是中國建政七十週年、西藏拉薩事件六十週年、八九六四屠城三十週年，也是香港多事之秋的一年。二〇一九年農曆新年過後，香港的《逃犯條例》修訂建議出爐，這「政治核彈」，轟爆香港原有的核心價值──香港人可被「送中」審理違反國家安全的案件。往後的二〇一九年，一百萬、兩百萬人站出來遊行，向專制政權說不，而「光復香港、時代革命」以及「願榮光歸香港」，把跨世代的香港人團結在一起，向不守信用的極權作對沖抗衡。

時光再「快閃」到現在的二〇二四。過去四年，在「港版國安法」實施下，香港人為了逃避共產黨，到處漂泊，一部份人落腳到臺灣、英美加澳紐等地。香港人不懂政治，但政治始終要埋身（你不理政治，政治依然會找上你）。而自二〇二二年開始，世界聚焦於俄羅斯和烏克蘭；二〇二三年尾，恐怖組織哈馬斯突襲以色列，中東局勢以致全世界的和平穩定都亮起了紅燈。

如無意外，此書將於臺灣總統大選前後出版。我沒有水晶球，但願臺灣新的總統，給亞洲以致全世界一個很好的示範：人口不多的國家，能夠做出超乎想像的大事：臺灣做到了，也可以更強大。過去近四年來，美國總統拜登政府涉入俄烏戰爭以及以色列與哈馬斯的「終極戰」。美國和中國長久的政治博弈，前總統特朗普會否重返白宮，全部有待分曉，結局難以預料。

其實，真正的貿易戰已經展開，資本已逃離中國，而新加坡、臺灣、越南及柬埔寨受惠。

二〇二四並沒有「世界第三次大戰」，只有更複雜的「政治博弈」。一九五九年到現在，是西藏抗暴六五周年，有多少人聯想到一九五一年西藏和中國簽署的《十七條協議》，以及一九八四年中國和英國簽署的《中英聯合聲明》，其實大有雷同？中共在一九五九年「大開殺戒」，進入西藏布達拉宮企圖「抓捕」十四世達賴喇嘛尊者；八九六四屠城，中共近乎已成功在中國境內把這「記憶禁區」抹去，只有香港、臺灣及世界各地有華人的地方，依然堅持。香港二〇一九年的反修例事件，被中共藉機定性為「暴亂」，而二〇二四年，香港除了港版國安法，還將會加入二十三條。基本上，香港的出版自由、資訊自由以及網路自由，將會「完全走向大陸化」。中國經濟下滑，習近平「武統臺灣」的口號，結局同樣難以預料，而世界就是存在著兩個對立面：西方的普世自由價值 vs. 極權專制政權。

我從事金融操作已有四分之一個世紀，對民主自由的熱衷，由低度到積極參與，同樣超過

四分之一個世紀。因國安法下，包括筆者在內，很多家庭也出現了變化。我不是白手興家，不是做實業，也不懂得製造一個物件出來；只想從絕對回報技巧中，利用金錢槓桿的特性尋找獲利機會。時移勢易，不懂得AI人工智能、區塊鏈及加密貨幣背後的意義將會與時代脫節。以前少受教育的人謂之「文盲」，現在的文盲則是指不懂使用電腦，不懂得簡易程式編寫的人。

在金融圈四分之一個世紀，身家上的漲跌是無可避免的事情；香港及海外資產泡沫膨脹，許多有物業的香港人曾經變成美元計的百萬富翁；快轉到二〇二四，高利息環境下，高槓桿比率的「樓奴」有些淪為負資產，也不快樂。不同的資產類別曾經「升到無朋友」，現在樓價不斷調整，又有多少人願意在此刻蝕錢出場，承認自己新家大縮水？

過去數年，最大的衝擊，就是香港人在「主旋律」操控下，變了「大灣區‧香港人」，受到強力監控，也失去言論自由。政治、金融、經濟及民生其實一環扣一環，而香港人歷經一次又一次的「身份改變」，令不少人有不同的體會，從而調整自己的想法。

絕對回報是鬥智鬥力的遊戲，我喜愛參與其中。但坦白說，十年如一日的投資生涯，真是沒有多大意義，特別當我進入了人生下半場的「上場」後，我更加有這種強烈感覺。五十知天命，這個「死線」，五年多前，已順利降臨到筆者身上；舊事已成過去，新的事情從頭開始。

金融操盤原本是我的主軸，但香港巨變，最有能力的人身陷獄中，筆者對餘下人生的「使命」

也有不同的領悟，唯有待香港政治犯「發聲」，從世界各地聲援，繼續說香港的真正故事。

《對沖人生路 自由價更高》這書的構思其實是「先談及自由與公義，然後分享健康與投資。全天候性的操盤運作，長短均可；在短暫的人生當中，如何善用數萬天；是整個人生的策略和使命。」文章內容，以英語及正體中文字為主軸，涉及我對香港、中港臺以至世界局勢的看法。中文和英文的內容，不會翻譯，原文出版。

筆者特別把這書獻給支持自由、理想、創意、普世價值、敢於發聲的地球村人。與此同時，筆者也想獻給我的母親 Dr. Doreen Chin 及兒子 Nathan 作為紀念。多謝母親把我帶到世上，永遠默默支持我。對於小兒 Nathan，我希望他能在愛中成長；也願以此書作為歷史的見證，將二〇一四及二〇一九年的香港大事，不模糊地傳開去。

筆者的經驗，或許也是一小撮在香港從事金融業，但堅持民主自由人士的經歷吧？筆者除了四分之一世紀的操盤經驗，在現時「習近平思想及管治權永續」的狀況下，對於金融、政治、經濟、流亡及人生已有全然不同的新體會。

香港人已變成「世界的香港人」。香港人絕大部份不能欣然接受香港變得只是「中國的另一個城市」。我們在賺錢及求存的同時，不要忘記我們的初心。鄧小平曾經說過的「一國兩制」，這個實驗是否已經蕩然無存，徹底失敗？還可以馬照跑、舞照跳、無牽無掛地活著嗎？

筆者歡迎你用電郵與我聯絡：edckchin@gmail.com，金融以外的天空可以很廣很闊，賺錢以外，捍衛及傳承香港的核心價值尤其重要。

錢志健 Ed Chin

二〇二四年一月八日　星期一

目次

好評推薦／沈旭暉／003

序／曾振超／004

自序／錢志健／007

真的邁開走向更遠的路／017

中共強權下的港澳疆藏／019

中共病毒，香港變天／022

股樓投資，低買高賣／024

香港已變，願來年更好／026

《小屋》：為何不幸降臨／028

龐貝奧的新書《一寸也不讓》及其它／031

戴教授背負的十字架／034

四十七人案的極權大審判／037

第三次世界大戰熱身戰／039

戰地孤聲，人生如戲／041

中共港共，好識得玩！／043

基努・李維 vs.甄子丹／045

義本無言，篤灰可恥／048

談惡意軟體：拼多多天美／050

西藏香港臺灣／053

香港已沒兩制，仍講馬照跑？／055

民主遊行已成絕響／057

致富心態，貪錢作怪／059

香港噤聲下，人財兩空／061

港共表忠，民主國家不可裝睡／063

一年已巨變，何況已三年？／065

港股變天，勇氣不滅／068

高機率投資，尋獲利之道／070

世界的香港，最後守護者／072

香港有儂味，這個夏天螞蟻搬家／075

香港曾是強力品牌／077

香港笑不出，七一好安靜／080

大灣區香港人／083

香港並非無藥可救／085

香港迎接各種波動／087

一國兩制，一切幻影／089

獄中贈畫，人間有情／092

香港被清洗，政敵被死亡／094

一國兩制還可捍衛？／097

傾國家力量治理香港／098

世上沒有發達祕笈／100

APEC峰會，世界在看／102

年尾收爐，命運在手／104

香港大崩壞，自由價更高／106

真的邁開走向更遠的路

那個週一，我從加拿大東岸攝氏十五度的多倫多來到負十七度嚴寒天氣的卡加利，出席了資深評論員及作家李怡前輩的追思會與葬禮。所有事情一如加拿大東西兩岸的溫度，有著強烈對比。在追思會中，一些熟悉的名字不能親身到來，在場嘉賓讀出這些未能出席朋友的心聲。程翔及黃毓民很有心，追思李怡生前的點點滴滴，最重要的，是談及李怡對民主及自由反思。

令我最為感動的，是李怡的長女，說到黎智英先生畫給李怡的一幅掃描：基督釘在十字架的情景。追思會歷時大約四十五分鐘；而李怡前輩的骨灰，安葬在愛妻旁邊，場面溫馨。對於有天主教和基督教信念的朋友，其實李怡只是返回天家。

離開，是為了走更遠的路。自二〇一九年返修例運動至現在，多少人顛沛流離。過去一年多，和一些年輕「手足」在英美加互動，離開「時代革命」的場景三年後，他們如何看待未來？今日不知明日事，但日子點都要過。其實現在，英美加澳紐臺這些國家，經過這幾年香港人的「大遷徙」，已有不同社群聯結著香港族群。

今天特別想分享加拿大的 Stream A 及 Stream B 計劃。A 和 B 不同之處，就是 A 計劃是先讀

書，再申請移民。B計劃是申請工作簽證。還未離開香港的朋友，如果想「走更遠的路」，可參考加拿大的「救生艇」計劃，充分了解是否符合各自的需要。最近認識有位朋友，已經六十二歲，將會參與A計劃。十六個月的認可「短期課程」，足以改變人生。

香港已變。不少評論人，無論財經或政治，已經「封筆」。二十大過後，香港更見極權。傳媒及評論，是現在政權重點打壓的對象，從正常的金融角度看香港，其實也已不可能，當每件事都要「表忠」，已是不正常的社會。

二○二三年十一月二十二號，蘋果日報高層開審，壹傳媒創辦人黎智英，則在十二月一號開審，形勢大大不妙。國安大法無極限，香港人更要盼望有奇蹟，才可渡過全方位的「難關」，這是漫長歲月的博弈。香港現時淪落到每一份政府主要職位、公職都要「上面」祝福；在沒有泛民議員的監察下，香港已經返智到任何事情都要作自我審查。

金融及領袖高峰會結束，只能以鬧劇一場來形容。中共港共當然不認為自己搞死香港，中共是要透過各種方法全面管治香港，其實香港已不再一樣。引用聖經金句：「那美好的仗，我已經打過了；該跑的路程，我已經跑盡了；當守的信仰，我已經持守了。」離開香港，是為了走更遠的路。

中共強權下的港澳疆藏

澳門，本來是「小城故事」，地方少，賭枱多，一些賭枱銀碼可以很大。但在疫情下，酒色財氣生意淡薄。至於香港，經歷了二〇一九年的時代革命，已變成超級人工智能監控城市，沒有回頭路。愛國者治港下，批判聲音被「清零」。香港現在多區有無數的智能燈柱，再加上人臉識別，市民的每個動作盡在掌握之內。蘋果日報被結束，再沒有監察政府的傳媒可言，港澳兩地，變得極為「馴服」了。

習近平曾經評價澳門比香港「更乖」，其實這說法沒有什麼大意義。香港人仍憧憬鄧小平「馬照跑、舞照跳，罵共產黨也可以」的思維構圖，因為香港人深信批判聲音的寶貴。然而過去兩年半，在無敵國安法下，香港人「投奔怒海」；二十大後，香港未見政治鬆綁，公民社會完全崩潰，任何眾籌集資活動，在未來一年，相信也會消聲匿跡。

二〇二三年也是西藏抗暴六十三週年。這是一九五九，中國共產黨入侵西藏，進行滅絕式清洗，再有教育營。自一九五一年西藏及中國簽署的「十七條協議」，西藏遭受的殘酷統治，實在是難以想像。六十三年後，曾經神聖的西藏布達拉宮，已成為遊客區。西藏人的壓抑，普

通人難以想像；一小撮人民最終走上「自焚」之路，但又何曾得到世界真正的關注呢？莫忘鄧小平同樣曾在一九八〇年代和位於印度的西藏流亡政府展開「和談」，談了十五年也沒有結果；二〇〇八年後，中共已對西藏建議的「中間路線」不理不睬。現在的西藏，漢人主導，西藏人的優秀兒童被送往北京接受黨的「教育」，在黨的「悉心栽培」下再派駐西藏，管治原有強烈藏傳佛教色彩的當地藏人。真正的西藏歷史、宗教、文化及語言，現在只能在印度北面的達蘭薩拉，現在的西藏流亡政府所在地才可感受到。至於新疆，集中營扣押回教徒，把不能容易抽出的避孕環放進新疆婦女體內，減少族群延續下一代的可行性，惡行令人咋舌。

現在的香港，同樣自幼稚園開始，就「被教育」要有「愛國情操」，並出現了不文明的「未審先扣押」，政治不正確，就可能涉嫌違反國安法、顛覆國家政權。香港被殖民、被換血，「維穩工程」積極進行中，但會否如像西藏一樣悲情，最終連文化及語言都被毀滅？真正的「舊香港」，市民內心始終是充滿熱誠、懷抱對明天的信念的，；然而今天多少人是意興闌珊，萌生移民或再移民的念頭。

在新聞自由方面，根據《無國界記者》的資料，中共政權在中港兩地便逮捕高達一百一十人入獄，而全球新聞工作者坐監人數一共只五百三十三人。極權中國扣押的新聞工作者人數，比起緬甸多出更多。

香港現已由「半威權」走向極權，變為一個警察都市，這是客觀事實。打沉香港人意志的方法層出不窮，香港的獨特性慢慢地消失，正在被摧毀。北京應當明白，香港人需要公平競爭、保障司法獨立，而非北大人所追捧的「三權合作」。香港怪象，已淪落到難以筆墨形容的地步。我看到的「香港風險」就是此地變得非常安靜，異常「恐怖地安靜」。想想香港有民主改變的一代全被ＤＱ入獄。香港已快要只剩下一個「虛殼」。

中共病毒，香港變天

二〇二二年十二月二十八日，《彭博》引述報導，在兩班由中國飛往意大利米蘭的飛機中，百分之五十的乘客感染了新冠病毒，數字令相當嚇人。由動態清零到一百八十度轉彎、晦氣地的完全開放，中國現在估計有二億多人患上武漢肺炎。二〇二三年中國大陸與香港由上而下完全開關，預計香港的醫療系統將會崩潰。世界對中國的做法不敢掉以輕心。

全世界現在對中國、香港、澳門預計將會「一視同仁」。有朋友買了香港去日本轉機，落腳點是加拿大溫哥華的機票，現在要退票。日本對中港澳的大門是否很快全封？如果各國預防措施不足，中共病毒遲來的「大爆發」將會佔領全世界。有評論指，這是中共二〇二三年的「生化武器」，也好像《葉問》電影橋段中，一個打百個。至於在香港，目測可見，藥房的退燒藥，在一些地方，已經加價幾倍，好像發「死人財」一樣。

至於中國內地民眾，預計將會洶湧至香港打疫苗。「世界級」的陸人，順道處理在香港的個人資產，先套現，再把資產轉移海外。網上這樣瘋傳，中港開關後，香港人回內地探親，把新冠病毒傳到國內，中共病毒的「源頭」找到替死鬼，問題可以解決。

香港問題多的是，二〇二三年將會面臨倒閉潮及失業潮。四十七人案、支聯會及蘋果日報黎智英案，將會成為下一年的焦點。Tim Owen 海外大律師是否可代表黎智英已非重點，過去兩年，自港版國安法實施下，強權暴政，令世界投資者對香港失去信心才是首重。香港國安法下，令人感覺法治倒退一百五十年，也令世界投資者對香港失去信心；「釘官」尤如內地，被定罪的機率幾近百分之九十九．九九。

一國兩制的下半場，情況坎坷。至於人大釋法，已經列入議程。二〇二二年常常聽到的口頭禪是要全方位的「堵塞漏洞」，更多自由將會失去。金融地產方面，賣樓套現，仍然持續。信心與人心是互動的，現在全方位的「被佔領」，每個人都可能踩地雷，涉及「危害國家安全罪」。二〇二二年，最常聽到第一句話似乎就是「好想移民，但有能力走」。最近和一位八十一歲，來加拿大，透過救生艇 Stream A 讀書的老太太互動。才發現，原來離開真的是為了走更遠的路。今天的離開，是為了明天的回來。老太善用了加拿大讀書「救生艇」，以及高齡，仍重新學習新事物，是堅持，也是樂趣。祝未來一年，大家一起繼續沉著面對，勇往直前。香港人加油；世界的香港，如何建立，全賴有你！

股樓投資，低買高賣

過往的投資模式，是否就是一成不變？美國聯儲局主席鮑威爾日前講話，必須壓抑通脹，加息周期仍然持續。這對定息投資相對有利。上世紀八〇年代初期，一些有錢的中產，經歷了「食息」也可安享晚年的好年華。加拿大的銀行收息股，過去是一些投資者的「寵兒」，沒有像美國投資次貸市場（案：又稱次按市場），需要美國政府挽救。任何投資，自己必需努力研究。

加密貨幣投機炒賣，某程度上因為 FTX 交易平臺的倒閉，這個市場跌得一仆一碌。當你去到一些地方，一些機器可以買 Bitcoin，但入得唔出得，再變回實質貨幣卻是相對困難，這不是一般投資者的「那杯茶」。Coinbase 宣布大裁員，現在的說法是虛擬貨幣這個 asset class 汰溺留強，但筆者真的看不通，仍然還是那句老話：遠離一些自己不明白的 business model。

科技股是極具波幅的股票類別：PE 值高的股票，在公司還有前途時，甚至去到一百倍 PE，股價也可上升，直至商業模式，已經屬於「非高增長」，股價可以急速下跌。股市當然也可以是人為，報復式買賣，我們也曾經見過。CNBC 財經頻道也報導過 N 次一些細價股或大藍籌股票，有「新消息」的時候，可能引致炒賣活動，我們叫它做 "inplay"。

芝加哥波幅指數 VIX 期指或期權，在專業投資者的領域，確實可以用來對沖「正股」的波幅。在專業投資者的領域，VIX 每一「大點」升跌代表一千美元，普通投資者「落注」十張，已經可以很大上落。普通人可上 CBOE.com 了解多一些 VIX 的操作辦法。在此補充一句：衍生工具，用作投機的，除非是專業投資者，個別人士「落重注」參與，多數衰收尾，真的毋須強求。

在政治動盪的時候，老牌投資者也會睇錯。當你見到市場上一些地產資深投資者，不斷在地產上沽貨套現，這是「亂世對沖」方法之一。你可有一萬個理由買樓自住，但看一九五〇年的上海，實業家幾經艱辛移居香港，大部份也是放棄家產，由零開始，來到英國殖民地管治下的香港。這是很淺易的道理：就算一無所有，他們見到當時的香港，就是有著「希望」。

最後，在新香港下，當我們見到壹傳媒急速「被停牌」，完全屬於政治事件，已令國際投資者明白，香港不是冒險家的樂園。國安法下，很多事情可以「特事特辦」，包括凍結資產，扣留你的護照、恐嚇，真的人生扣留。這種大環境下，令人想起中共的大躍進、文化大革命等。再遠的不說了，馬雲是黨員，現在真的「錢歸還於黨」，誰能不被「清零」？由有到冇，我們更應看到當中的「政治暴力」，令人不寒而慄！

香港已變，願來年更好

二〇二三的農曆年前，國安警察高調出動，全力掃蕩「隱世市集」。據報導指，參展商有售賣「煽動性刊物」，這在新香港管治模式下，紅線點樣定，真的很難講。現在每講一句話，在香港都要很小心，或很有「技巧」。中國大陸的「白紙革命」，已拘捕若干人「祭旗」，他們也可能是「顛覆國家政權」，不知道需要坐牢十年八載，還是終身監禁。

香港價值，本應就是多元化，多批判，這才令香港紮實。如今香港要被急速改變，生意風險，更要了解到 rules of the game 已大大不同，全方位價值，已被中國大陸化。法律界二〇二三新一年度開啟，各大持份者一於歌頌習近平。不少專業團體，也是 self regulated 自我規管的；但在現今的香港，行外人管行內人，最終搞個大頭佛。

當香港的司法獨立，三權分立已被世界質疑；原來香港人的自由，正如某「吹水代理人」所講，也非絕對的，那麼在香港能夠呼吸，是否需要「謝主隆恩」？這些文革風，這麼癲的香港，原來出自「愛國者」，這樣的演繹，嚇壞全世界。

在二〇一九年逃犯條例修訂爭拗，到二〇一九自由之夏；二〇二〇年國安惡法壓下，「文

革改造」已近乎把香港整死。假如時光倒流到二〇一九，這樣的震懾，足以有數百萬人上街了。現在香港已經滅聲，我的建制「半生熟」之交，身體最誠實，過去兩年已大舉撤退，再次移走，螞蟻搬家。二〇二三年的農曆新年，離開香港的人數創新高，也是意料中事。二十三條立法在即，最高刑罰是終身監禁。再加上港版國安法，基本上香港已變了「隨時踩地雷」的恐怖都市。；反抗就是罪名，思想如不正確，在灰色地帶遊走，最終插翅難飛。

已故的鄧小平，就是希望香港有不同的聲音。已仙遊的自由黨創黨主席李鵬飛、李柱銘及黎智英，捍衛了香港多年的民主及法治與自由，所謂的「外國勢力」，才會有信心來香港，深信一國兩制存在。香港的悲劇，是政權把黎智英當作「第一類重犯」，其實如果沒有黎智英先生及壹傳媒，回歸後捱不了這麼二十三年。如果沒有這個橫空出世的國安法，黎智英就是可以競逐特首其中一人；前財爺曾俊華也將會是不錯的選擇；如果香港有真正的選舉，榮休的政協劉夢熊也會是不錯的選擇。

《港版國安法》在黎智英先生案件當中，凸顯了香港現有的「政治暴力」，香港已不再安全。現在失控的香港，也徹底破壞了鄧小平在六四悲劇後，修補世人對中華人民共和國以及香港特別行政區的看法。四十七人案現正開審，這是全世界的最焦點。願來年會更好！

《小屋》：為何不幸降臨

一個更高層次的付出，可從黎智英先生看到。十二歲從廣州經澳門到香港，開始了他的製衣事業，為六四，再轉至傳媒。從行到有，變了一個億萬富豪，上市公司主席，被殘酷政權「推落山」，這是世界已經看到，但還看不清楚的事實。法律學者戴耀廷，同樣受到我無比的尊重。沒有人想到，香港除了金融褪色，法治也絕對崩壞了。

我沒有家世背景，在前半生，因為機緣際遇，開始了金融事業，以及半途出家，也接觸了廣播事業。人生上半場已經走完，下半場卻遇上了損害「一國兩制」的《港版國安法》降臨香江。人生下半場需要花心力、時間及資源，好好「回饋」監獄中的「義士」。講完一輪開場白，以下幾本好書，將會為大家作很好的心靈排毒：

（一）*The Shack* 《小屋》，by William Paul Young。這暢銷小說數年前拍成電影，我也曾經看過，故事激勵人心。內容講述一位普通父親，在夏令營中眼見女兒在湖邊的渡假屋消失了。故事主角知道女兒遇害，他獨自返回《小屋》山上的凶案現場，質問上帝為何不幸的事情落在他身上。他和上帝的「互動」，令他得到一個奇妙之旅。

現實版《小屋》的作者 William Paul Young 更具傳奇。生於加拿大的傳教士家庭，幼年隨父母至新幾內亞傳教，卻在當地的部落與寄宿學校遭到長期性侵。十歲時全家回到加拿大，父親往返各地巡迴宣教，因此他在高中畢業前一共轉了十三間不同的學校。成年後 Paul Young 經過婚外情的考驗，以及投資失利、破產等人生關卡，在低潮時曾與妻兒在「劏房」居住，做多份工作養家，並接受心理治療，努力與家人修補關係。

Paul Young 在《小屋》出版前近乎身無一文。他自費印刷了十五本以後，有好友鼓勵他找出版社出書，卻遭到二十六家出版社拒絕，於是他們在二〇〇七年決定自行創立 Windblown 出版社來發行《小屋》。誰也沒想到的是，這本僅花了三百美金宣傳的小說，口碑絕好，出版十三個月便售出一百一十萬冊，接著在《紐約時報》暢銷榜長踞冠軍達一年之久。如今，《小屋》已經在全球翻譯為五十種語言出版，銷售破兩千萬冊。

（二）*Chasing Daylights, by Eugene O'Kelly*。健康第一，錢財第二？活在當下，還是要拚，去到最後一口氣？成功的人士，大多數更是 family first，否則失去更多。古語有云，金錢是萬惡之根，也令人脫離了真道。是否真的活到一百二十歲，一百二十五歲才說

「退休」？我沒有預知能力，其實沒有健康，有多少錢也沒有用。香港變得太快，是政經及民生的「壓力煲」；能在這裡「生存」，其實已不容易。四大會計師樓KPMG環球主席及CEO Eugene O'Kelly 在二〇〇五年五月，以五十三歲之齡發現患了腦癌。他沉默面對，用一百天的時間寫下傳記《追逐日光》（*Chasing Daylights*），同年十月十號離開人世。Eugene 的故事，在金融及專業人士領域，可能特別有共鳴。

（三）*God In My Corner, by George Foreman*。這位兩度世界拳王，曾經在非洲肯亞輸了拳賽給阿里。年輕時做奧運代表賺不到錢，成為世界拳王後不善理財，又輸到一仆一碌，最後被上帝感召，教邊緣青年打拳擊，最後成為廚房用品 George Foreman Grill 的KOL，搞好自身經濟環境，在一九九四年，即四十五歲高齡第二次榮登拳王寶座。原來人生的最高「層次」，並不是金錢和名利，而是在上帝的引領下，活出真意義。

龐貝奧的新書《一寸也不讓》及其它

美國前國務卿龐貝奧 Mike Pompeo 的新書《一寸也不讓》（*Never Give An Inch: Fighting For The America I Love*）在二〇二三年一月剛面世。電子版，十六美元，硬皮精裝版二十一美元。假如大家已經習慣在 YouTube 接受政治或時事資訊，龐貝奧這半新書，坦白說，恍如一股清泉，令大家更加明白到，美國如何看國家安全，以及前美國總統在外交上，一些些想法。龐貝奧是軍人出身，在哈佛法學院畢業，曾經在特朗普任總統期間，做過中央情報局ＣＩＡ的第一把交椅，在成為美國國務卿。

《一寸也不讓》是從美國的角度，看整個世界。習近平、普京及北韓金正恩，在這位前國務卿眼中，是世界上最危險的三個人。金融大鱷索羅斯，同樣把習近平形容為「極危險人物」。美國政治，去到最後，講求民主及核心價值。書中提到現在已被涉嫌違反國安法的陳日君樞機、黎智英，以及民主黨創辦人李柱銘等香港人認識的名字，花了很大的篇幅。龐貝奧明白要把中共和中國人分開來看，專制政權最終會大敗。這是一本「實戰」的好書，因為全是一手的江湖經驗。

第二本要介紹的好書，是用來「對沖」投資者在二○二二年的「損手爛腳」經驗。上年，投資科技股，確實書道一仆一碌；虛擬貨幣買賣，風險難以評估。美國標普及道指以及科技股為主打的納斯達克指數，走勢反覆。電動車如特斯拉，臉書母公司 Meta，也有接近七成的回調，整個二○二二年，相當之嚇人。

接觸投資及絕對回報領域已有四分一個世紀，除了要學習紮實的操作及分析技巧，鑽研不同的書本可以彌補金融以外，很多需要理解的事情。讓筆者介紹一本歷久常新的好書 One Up On Wall Street，作者是「神級」傳統基金經理彼德‧林治（PeterLynch）。此書之前也有介紹，其重要性，好像如對沖基金對沖基金之神索羅斯的《金融煉金術》（The Alchemy of Finance）．

Peter Lynch 在他的投資哲學中，要尋找罕有的「寶藏」，就要從日常生活開始。某些知名的品牌，有不同的增長期，若在適當時段作中、長線投資，是建倉的根基。市場上「十倍奉還」股（Ten Bagger），就是由他所創。此書百看不厭，更重要的是，書裡鑽研建倉理論與實踐，與香港操盤人鍾情於股票死炒爛炒，此書突顯了他和炒友的強烈對比。

最後一本要介紹的好書，是二○二二年出版的 Today Hong Kong, Tomorrow The World，而作者是蘋果日報的前上市公司董事 Mark Clifford。書本的精要，講及中共「改造香港」的大計畫。

筆者有幸在書本的第二章出現，講及為何金融人要撐「和平佔中」，再回顧至二○二○年六月

三十號晚上十一時至現在，香港「根本性」的變化。其實可以肯定，一國兩制已經名存實亡，在「偽兩制」的運作下，香港難以復原。

戴教授背負的十字架

不敢說什麼萬世流芳，也不敢說流芳百世。二〇一三至二〇一四年，主力醞釀和平佔中的戴耀廷教授，在推動香港民主的領域上，打了一場美好的仗。中國現在經濟「爛到痺」，香港財赤也嚴重，中美博弈，香港首當其衝。在一個極權當道，沒有制衡的社會，人民最終被欺壓。極左路線佔領香港，極權把所有義人拉了，戴教授未審先判接近兩年，罪名是「顛覆國家政權」，而他由始至終就只是一位講真話、捍衛「一國兩制」的學者。

戴教授沒有被提名諾貝爾和平獎，令我感到詫異。話雖如此，被提名的六人：陳日君、樞機、黎智英、李卓人、鄒幸彤、何桂籃，香港人絕對熟悉；而戴耀廷教授在四十七人案件中是D1，中共的眼中釘，也是最捍衛「一國兩制」的先鋒；他是「一國兩制」《香港基本法諮詢委員會》當年的學生代表之一。在四十七人案當中的「冤獄」，戴耀廷教授「被釘十架」；以往戰友因做污點證人可獲輕判或無罪釋放，這個不可能的任務他「完成了」，如果說他要交代，那是對上帝的交代。這樣的高尚情操，如同被釘十字架。戴耀廷不喜出風頭，但時代揀了他「和平佔中」，大家不要忘記，他為香港已付出了一切。

雷動計劃、風雲計劃或和平佔中也好，戴耀廷教授所推動的，是在「一國兩制」框架下，一人一票選特首的運作模式。強權壓下，中共沒有做到給香港人及世界的承諾，即港人治港、高度自治。最悲慘的實況，就是一百八十度地改變鄧小平的構思。如果香港有真正的民主，戴耀廷教授將會是最好的律政司司長人選。他在香港大學法律系的同級同學，有前律政司司長袁國強、法律學者張達明、投入新聞界的劉進圖；有人走向建制，有人捍衛媒體，但現在所有曾經是香港紮實的根基，也崩壞了。

最多人認識戴教授的時候是二○一三至二○一四年，和平佔中的醞釀期及至運動的終結，即二○一四年九月二十六號。往後的九二八，已經變成雨傘運動，以年青人為主導。現在中共港共玩的政治遊戲，就是找最有影響力的人「祭旗」。九十天的公審，在國安大法下，徹底毀滅「一國兩制」的初心。原本應有的「港法治港」，變為中國特色「法治」，即極權管治，也把鄧小平原先的構思「釘蓋」。

不義之審判，全世界都有。非洲獨裁國家、現今的緬甸，案例、數不勝數。國安大法以「國家安全」之名，扼殺所有反對聲音。無論你是泛民、本土、個別獨立，支持民主的參與者，只要參加「民主派初選」，便會惹來「殺身之禍」。假如香港有真民主，美帝也不會放棄香港這個曾經的金融中心⋯⋯馬照跑、舞照跳，罵共產黨也沒有什麼大不了。在中美博弈下，

香港政治犯的最終結局難料。香港進入「終極大審判」之年。二〇一九年社會事件的「領頭人」，正接受不義之審。處理方法，沒有最荒謬，只有更荒謬。希望各人捱得住悲痛的日子，盼望將會有最終的「勝利」。

四十七人案的極權大審判

一場不公義的四十七人案，意味著香港正式進入「中國特色」法庭審判。民意是中共港共政權最不想面對的客觀現實。香港現在所有主要決定，以政治行先，情何以堪。泛民陣營的內部初選，由合法變為非法，相當之嚇人。

四十七人案審訊的第十天，我再沒有太大的心力等待四位「污點證人」出庭「篤灰」。在聖經當中，猶大出賣了耶穌，而「上帝之子」為眾人攬罪上身，拯救世人。四十七人案件，社會運動家其實也是「萬箭穿心」，沒有一個值得被監禁，未審先囚，歷史必定會為他們作一個公道定案。

在沒有陪審團的情況下，極權本來想「假戲真做」，但始終是「假戲假做」，因為情節太核突；有極權無公理。在極權世界，除了使用暴力鎮壓，還要把反對聲音鏟平，一切變得「平靜」。我們必須明白，極權政府，至少放棄了兩代人。

四十七人案的「污點證人」因國安法下，無法避免法律責任，被扣押的有三人已近兩年失去自由。審訊的第九天，我們知道「控方證人」（Prosecution Witness）區樂軒自前年九月已協

助警方調查。未來至少八十天審訊，還有趙家賢的供詞，也會成為大家的焦點。

整個香港，不知不覺「被改造」。以往在香港的金融界，分析員回中國內地不敢用回鄉證，而是用外國護照，便是因為對「內地法」的信心不足。在只可「唱好」的大前提下，如果分析報告中「唱淡」出問題的民企國企，會否也要被扣查？現在，香港已被噤聲，大行的主要人員，為了避開政治風險，大多移居新加坡。港版國安法，你話佢點好，已經唔重要；講都冇人信，建制先走佬。一些「榮休」的人大政協，現在不斷在英國加拿大「蒲頭」購買當地房地產，這和「說好香港故事」完全背道而馳。我仍然相信，有健全的司法制度，真正的三權分立，投資者便會回來。這個「整頓香港人」的無極限國安大法，已經活生生埋葬了「一國兩制」，未來的二十四年多，偽一國兩制下半場，沒有最差，只有更差。

二○二二年有六萬香港人「淨移出」海外，真的「說好香港故事」？國安法實施到現在，香港已成為真正的「軍管城市」。全世界也看到中共港共的干預已成習慣，由「高度干預」變了「全面管治」，香港的獨特性，已沒有真價值。李家超為首的特區政府，已令香港這個曾經的國際城市付上沉重的代價。

第三次世界大戰熱身戰

現時的地緣政治局勢正在升級中，一些分析員把它形容為準戰爭狀態。烏克蘭有美國及北大西洋公約組織 NATO「撐腰」，除了戰鬥機，這場戰爭可以持續一段時間。烏克蘭被俄羅斯入侵的一周年，中共當時的外交部長王毅正在莫斯科，而美國總統拜登和烏克蘭總統澤連斯基在烏國首都基輔發表演講。中共試圖扮演「和平使者」的角色，全世界都關注習近平是否會到莫斯科發表講話。

世界的邪惡軸心，是否變成中俄北韓與伊朗？習近平及整個中共宣傳體系譴責美國的「霸權主義」，要他們莫對他國外交事務指指點點。對於美國而言，國務卿布林肯已多次強調，中共如果為俄羅斯提供支援，將會有「嚴重後果」。伊朗的無人偵察機被指用在俄烏戰爭當中。

同一時間，香港人的關注面，可能是財政司長各類型的「派糖」行動。但五千港幣的消費券，卻是難以減輕港版國安法實施後，港人完全噤聲的那種失去自由的無奈。大家不要忘記，當北京決定二〇二〇年六月實施港版國安法後，一切已經不能逆轉。從香港人的角度，無

被西方世界制裁的俄羅斯，不知什麼原因，超級遊艇竟可公然停泊在香港水域內？

論現居香港或海外，必須了解到「亂世對沖」的重要性。香港人的政治意識向來相當薄弱，未來必須特別關注地緣政治的變化。

在個人及公司資產的領域，由於港版國安法真的是「無極限」，香港的司法獨立，也存在疑問。匯豐銀行在政治壓力下，受制於香港的法律，假如你是「涉嫌觸犯國安法」，資產容易受到動機。前立法會議員許智峯事件，家人及個人資產受到凍結，銀行的環球 CEO Noel Quinn 也曾經為此事被英國的議員質詢，但結論是「無能為力」。香港現在最大的問題是，任何的商業行動，在頭頂上都多了一把刀。

我認識的建制半生熟之交，都了解假若突發大事出現，香港的「資金外流」將更加充滿不穩定性。戰爭，特別是指除了經濟戰，中共的實體「攻臺」，也會令香港處於極之不利的位置。會否出現資金管制、把不同光譜與理念的香港人「隔離」處理、實行宵禁，這並非無稽之談。再想下去，實在太恐怖了。

俄烏之戰踏入一周年，「攻臺」的後果究竟有多嚴重？地緣政治複雜，香港的「政治犯」也可能隨著政治變化，在危機中或可得到轉機。華為的孟晚舟和加拿大兩位 Michaels，最終「交換人質」解決紛爭，香港現在的政治犯被囚禁近兩年，能夠釋放與否，如何釋放，或也充斥著無限可能！

戰地孤聲，人生如戲

日前看了《戰地孤聲》的試片，英文片名是 Broken Keys，是一部翻譯電影。故事講述二○一三至二○一四年的中東，在敍利亞的戰亂中，一位鋼琴家為了修補一台被機關槍掃射摧毀的鋼琴，排除萬難所發生的故事。

此片探索了「活著」的重要性：今天不知明天事，還是積極面對每一天。在極權世界當中，人民變得鴉雀無聲。片中的恐怖組織 ISIS，依然存在，繼續橫行。敍利亞內戰是世界上最嚴重的人道主義災難。超過一半的敍利亞人被迫逃離家園，產生超過五百五十萬名難民。

現在更多人關注的，可能是俄烏戰爭。因為牽連甚廣，這包括中國作為泱泱大國，究竟背後有沒有向俄羅斯提供致命武器、協助攻打烏克蘭軍火，對抗俄羅斯入侵；中國卻不可以支援俄羅斯？王毅上周在慕尼黑問道，為何外國支援烏「腦殘」，不分是非黑白，也不知如何用筆墨形容這種思維了。這是大是大非的問題，除了說王毅

在現實世界，香港的情況絕對艱辛。共產黨透過國安法摧毀了香港珍貴的舊有核心價值。立法會前議員毛孟靜丈夫 Philip Bowring 病危，特區政府已經拘留毛孟靜兩年；現在英國五十四

名跨黨派議員以及末代港督彭定康致信英國外相，要求港府以人道理由，讓毛孟靜可以保釋外出，探望病危丈夫。數年前，我有份負責的二〇四七香港監察，在中環策劃了一論壇：「回歸二十年，清洗太平地」。左中右、淺藍黃、前立法會議員如梁繼昌、林卓廷、毛孟靜、前港區人大代表朱幼麟都有出席，我則作主持。剛才講述的議員，兩位在獄中，即毛孟靜及林卓廷。

開明建制派近乎全部收聲，香港進入恐怖政治。

香港曾經是國際都市，現在沒有各方平衡的聲音，只有單聲道。香港曾經是這樣多元化：生意佬及專業人士，有錢無錢，也可發聲。現在的軍管狀態，嚇壞資本家，個個尋出路。香港「防衛網」被攻破，這也是不爭的事實。舊有的香港，厚待了不少人，現在香港出現逃亡潮，歷史被改寫中。強權壓迫下，違背了鄧小平「一國兩制」一．〇的構思及實踐。中共港共不斷收緊香港，而四十七人案也進入了更漫長的審訊。

最後，香港已完全噤聲，海外則繼續有團體「幫真香港人出聲」，抗衡極權。香港警方國安處在二〇二一年逮捕五十三名民主派人士，指控他們策劃及參與二〇二〇年的民主派立法會初選，涉嫌違反《港區國安法》，其中四十七人被警方控告「串謀顛覆國家政權罪」當中多數被告，未經審判已先囚禁兩年。當香港只剩一種聲音，如果不同界別的人士依然裝睡，這才是最恐怖！

中共港共，好識得玩！

加拿大卡加利 Calgary，給人的印象是天寒地凍，寸草不生。夏天卻是酷熱，但以忍受。當香港正在審理四十七人案，立場新聞案及支聯會案件時，香港完全消音，海外城市接棒。卡加利人間有情，有著一群不拍寒冷，走到中領館門口，要求釋放政治犯的老華僑及新香港人，不斷發聲。

在加拿大，溫哥華及多倫多三地，也有中國領事館。不知是否存在「中國警察派出所」的關係，和平示威的人對中共戰狼「佔領加拿大」也提高了警覺。與此同時，根據加拿大國安情報局 CSIS 的調查顯示，中共滲透加拿大各級選舉的影響性，深入而長遠。現任總理杜魯多 Justin Trudeau，也是中共「心儀」的領袖，只要杜魯多所屬的自由黨，是小數黨。中共長臂，發揮了影響力。

中共戰狼，除了「鬧交部」——sorry，我指外交部；新紮政協，也搏命為共產黨作大外宣。藝人甄子丹，在外國媒體，發表了他「宇宙最強」宣言，聲稱二○一九年的社會運動，不是民主抗爭，而是暴動。隨之衍生的，就是網上有抗爭者「赴湯」，在 change.org 發起了「呼籲奧斯卡

金像獎評選會，撤回邀請甄子丹做頒獎嘉賓」的決定。下筆之時已有接近九萬人參與聯署。

前聯會主席李卓人因涉嫌違反國安法，已被扣留獄中。引述黨媒「文匯報」所了解，他的太太在二○二一年來開香港前往英國，星期四中午十二時許，在赤柱監獄探監後，便被國安處拘捕。不知道這是什麼「玩法」？在香港獄中的政治囚犯，已經坐了無謂的「政治監」太長太久了。不少「疑似」國安犯人，選擇認罪，也是正常不過。香港變得沒有程序，國安法凌駕一切，變得「無法無天」。整個「治港集團」，現在有了無限權力，用國家安全之名，可以長時間扣留無辜的人，這是名副其實的恐怖政治。

二○二三年的世界，大家感受到失去自由，我們活在極艱鉅的時刻。國安大法下，香港滅聲。由探監變成被拘捕、被還柙扣留，也算是香港的「特點」，唱好香港故事？在「維穩特首」李家超管治下，外資有不同的後著 contingency plan，香港自由不再。五十年不變行了一半，特區政府變為高壓政權，這是可怕的政治暴力。

在香港，去探監變成「被拉」，實屬罕見。自港版國安法實施下，強權暴政，令世界投資者對香港失去信心。香港國安法下，給人的感覺就是，香港的法治倒退一百五十年，也令世界投資者對香港失去信心。香港國安法下，被定罪機率，近乎百分之九十九・九九！

基努‧李維 vs. 甄子丹

一九六四年出生的「男神」基努‧李維（Keanu Reeves）和廣州出世、移居美國、香港成名的「宇宙最強」港區政協甄子丹（一九六三—）年紀相若，但在中港圈子、奧斯卡頒獎典禮上，卻來了一場激烈的 change.org「反對甄子丹作頒獎嘉賓」的網上投票戰。「反對甄政協」出席奧斯卡的網友，贏了一百條街。八九六四學運領袖王丹，就在奧斯卡頒獎典禮場外，為甄子丹「贈興」，抗議他為中共暴政抬橋。

對香港人而言，基努‧李維是《捍衛戰警》（又作《生死時速》）、*Matrix* 及 *John Wick* 殺神系列的主角。基努‧李維不是上一代動作巨星史特龍或阿諾史瓦辛格以肌肉見稱，有中國血統的他，可說是「帥哥」一名。前女友過世後，傳媒報導他依然孤獨接近二十年，到二〇一九才找到新的戀情。真與假，他自己才曉得。

基努‧李維的現任女友 Alex Grant 約在二〇一九年彼此「確認」；傳媒稱這位不修邊幅，會在紐約搭公車、出席粉絲「突襲」婚禮作嘉賓的他，是平凡中的不平凡。在公益的領域，基努‧李維在二〇二二年參與了在美國「西藏之家」的網上慈善音樂會。中國網民狠批，中國網

上娛樂串流公司一度下架他主演的作品，最後擺平。

基努‧李維支持西藏，代表他並非不明白地緣政治的風險。中國共產黨在一九五一年，強行逼西藏人簽署了《十七條協議》，一九五九年正式入侵西藏，達賴喇嘛十四世從此離開西藏，已經超過六十四年。一個政權，摧毀了另一個國家的宗教、文化及語言，這是中國以外地方，大部份人的認知。西藏是西藏，一九五九年，真的被中共入侵及佔領了。基努‧李維支持西藏相對低調，但在共產黨的眼中，挫擊「反對聲音」一個也不能少。他沒有像上一代的「男神」李察基爾（Richard Gere）般的被打壓，或許是市場使然？

至於李察基爾（一九四五─），對很多人來說，可能已是上一代人的「產品」。一九八〇年的 American Gigolo，一九九〇年的 Pretty Woman，到一九九七年的 Red Corner，李察基爾可說是上一代的「男神」。好萊塢需要龐大的中國市場支持，而李察選擇了支持西藏人的處境，荷里活不敢承受用他作為 A-list 的演員。李察在千禧年後，也受獨立製片商邀請演戲。或許情況就如香港的周冠威導演會找「黃圈」演員一樣，希望民主及公義，可以得到彰顯。

最後，也要一談甄子丹政協。坦白說，他也是很努力的演員，也許帶一點運氣，憑《葉問》走到人生演戲高峰。做政協，就是要政治協商，取了虛無飄渺的權力，放棄了香港人，如何支持以往舊有的「核心價值」。甄政協和習近平握手，不知他是否真的「鬆毛鬆翼」。

我相信如果是香港資金拍的電影，給香港人看的戲，從今以後，他會被「抵制」。他看到二〇一九年的社會運動，是百分之百的暴動，看不到香港人追求民主自由、爭取真普選的強烈訴求。願他的戲，可在中國國內大賣，做個真正「戰狼」內地演員，光復他的中國市場吧？

義本無言，篤灰可恥

前民主黨主席何俊仁涉嫌在國安法保釋期間，干擾證人而被捕。引述網上媒體《稜角》所指，同樣被國安箝制下的民主黨人趙家賢，因為何俊仁透過趙家賢太太「傳話」，叫趙「自保有問題」，憑良心說話」，因而「出事」。消息指趙家賢因「傳話」主動舉報國安。

何俊仁被取消保釋原因何在，沒有人能夠精準回答。在宇宙國安大法下，震懾性已把香港真的「震散」了。何俊仁和趙家賢同樣是前民主黨人，但沒有人想到，宇宙國安大法，把人與人之間的互信，降至到最低點。再聽到民主黨前黨員區諾軒，及阿布泰創辦人林景楠的「割蓆宣言」；認為黃色經濟圈，就是一個「錯誤的示範」，大家實在目瞪口呆。

現在香港的大環境，什麼事情都有不確定性。在絕望中，依然要有希望。這不是阿Q精神，只要還有一粒種子落在土壤，依然有著無限可能。先講政治大環境，何俊仁的處境已經和被扣查打壓的中國維權律師沒有差別。何俊仁的弟弟何俊麒，同樣受到打壓，唯一分別是可以保釋。

日前看到《東方日報》的標題，意思如下：超過一半的人，想離開香港，經濟壓力及政治壓

力的因素，超過百分之五十。不懂英語，也希望「闖出新世界」，這和李家超特首所說的「講好香港故事」背道而馳。當香港還有政治犯，實在不適宜國際投資者再放大量資源在這裡了。

在國際層面上，普京和習近平「稱兄道弟」，合作有底線。合作「沒有上限，沒有極限」令人困擾。中國如果和美國繼續處於「敵對」，又假如更多的證據顯示，在烏克蘭戰場上被擊落的無人偵察機，生產線來自大陸，下一步會是，美國制裁中國只會越來越激。中共權貴和美國人共通點不大，而不同背景的中國人「終極目標」就是成為美國公民。世界第一大黨的權貴資本往往會來到美加澳紐，而流動資金則更多落在離岸戶口。

在國際金融上，UBS 成為了白武士，挽救成為了白武士，挽救了 Credit Suisse，會否有更大的金融危機？暫時應該穩定。金錢遊戲，一切皆幻影。而在倒數中的香港，必須捍衛資產，保存實力。心態就是境界，世界政局不穩，但 panic sell 更加不理智。在倒數中的香港，炒賣可以好邪門，要有正確的態度，積極面對每一天。「目標回報」設定越高，風險部位也通常倍增。在政治壓力籠罩底下，投資是次要，自由價更高。我也會在此特別為高齡的香港政治犯祈禱。香港不需要更多的劉曉波或李旺陽死於非命。我仍相信，只要我們不放棄，香港的政治犯及整個香港，必然會有 set free 的一天。

談惡意軟體：拼多多天美

最近有位住在北美的朋友說，在TEMU 天美網上平臺買一些產品，然後在 Amazon 亞馬遜以更高價賣出，好像是沒有風險的套利交易，用對沖基金的術語，是 risk free arbitrage. 天美在中國的姊妹公司拼多多 Pin duo duo，在紐約納斯達克上市（PDD），市值約為九百四十億美元，算是在美國上市的中資概念「藍籌」股票，不太細。美國串流娛樂公司 Netflix（NFLX），現在市值約為一千五百五十億美元；而曾經是網上四大天王之一的 eBay，現在市值為兩百三十八億，不足拼多多市值的三分之一。

媒體ＣＮＮ日前出了報告，談到拼多多 App 這個應用程式出現了惡意軟件，即 Malware. 收集數據是包括美國在內，科技公司必然會作數據分析的指定動作。但 App 應用程式如果是「惡意」，可以令電腦網路等造成隱私或機密資料外洩、系統損害等「指定動作」。而科技巨人 Google，在三月尾已經停止拼多多在 android 系統下載這個 App。

在 Android 應用系統，當你下載了拼多多的 App，它便有能力繞過其他防禦系統，分析你手機中的其它 App，閱讀你的私人訊息，改變你的手機設定。這是一個很嚴重的問題。大家試

過當你公司電腦當機時，你可以叫 IT 部門切入你的電腦，看看有什麼「故障」。根據 CNN 的報導指，當你的手機或電腦被控制，你真的「大檸樂」了。我指的不只是你可能銀行戶口財產「被移走」，敵意系統也可把你整個人的 identity 嘥用。

CNN 的文章，只是提及天美 TEMU 為拼多多的姊妹公司。最近你在社交媒體頻繁見到 TEMU 的廣告，便宜到令人震驚的價錢，「精明消費者」大量下載 TEMU 的 App 平到震，其廣告如下：Shop Like A Billionaire——如億萬富豪般購物，這令我感到不安。

筆者再問了矽谷一位網路工程師，看到拼多多及 TEMU 的不少負面資料，真的要小心。至於惡意軟體 Malware，如果你已下載了應用程式，而尚未啟用或登記你的個人資料、串連信用卡，那麼是否會中伏？其實一旦下載程式到你的手機，就算你沒有開啟，如果是敵意軟體，你也已經「中伏」。你也必須更改所有電郵密碼，重新裝置電腦或手機的 O／S，別無他法。

至於銀行，可能你的密碼寫在手機 app 的 Note 內，你也必須做一個很痛苦，但必須做的「指定動作」，重新開戶，用一個全新的銀行戶口號碼。至於手機確認銀行密碼，由於舊的手機如果真的被 Malware 入侵，效果當然很嚴重。另一做法是改換新機。在此特別要談及 TEMU，這個在二〇二二年九月在北美洲推的 App，已有一些問題。一些不明來歷的「收費」，貨品直接由中國寄出，實質收不到。

至於 Spyware 間諜軟件則嚴重，請大家自己查閱，今日也不能詳細談論。但提醒大家，你可能最關心的銀行資料，密碼也被盜用。一些「鹹濕網站」，如果給你免費觀看下載，你也可能中伏了。曾經聽過，「受害者」再打去「中伏」後的拯救熱線：結果去了蘇聯。「受害者」和真人「技術員」對話，又給了對方信用卡資料去「解碼」，最終損失不只自己，連累「一村人」，請小心。筆者只是引述ＣＮＮ的報導及其他科技文章，每個用家或投資者，都必須不停地追問、不停地分析、不停地下結論，再作判斷。祝大家好運。

西藏香港臺灣

達賴喇嘛尊者十四世最近多了「麻煩」。保護兒童權益組織、國際傳媒，大肆報導。據了解，達賴喇嘛日前與一名印度男童的互動，當時除了親吻嘴唇，兩人額頭互碰，達賴喇嘛還對男童說「你可以吸我的舌頭」"suck my tongue"，那一名男童並沒有照做。

據了解，在西藏，伸出舌頭可以是一種問候方式；但在現今世代，這種文化表達也未必被接受，而達賴喇嘛十四世，也為此事即時公開道歉。筆者一直關注西藏議題，而西藏流亡議員達瓦才仁表示，「尊者希望向這個男孩及其家人，以及他在世界各地的許多朋友致歉。因為他的話可能造成傷害，尊者經常以天真及俏皮的方式與人互動，即使是在公開場合與鏡頭前也是如此，他對這起事件感到後悔。」

筆者此文首刊時，我應已拜訪過西藏基金會；這次「誤會」，真理會越辯越明。把話題延伸，現在西藏流亡政府，自一九五九年流亡政府的運行下，經歷了高低起跌，而目前在中國境外流亡的西藏人，不足八萬人。要了解西藏的歷史，你我更可以明白香港的處境。中共侵佔西藏的三部曲是：進入西藏、立足西藏、改造西藏（公路通車與一九五五年的西藏民主改革）。

大家明白，香港人在國安法下，已失去自由，各散東西。對未來，香港人必須明白一九五九年西藏被中共佔領後的這段悲慘歷史。香港人的信心已很薄弱，有部份可能「送中」，也怕財產、自由、人權在沒有保障及在恐懼中被奪去。找一個藉口，剝削了你我的生存權利，不斷「改造」、「取代」，香港舊有的核心價值，直至蕩然無存。這一點，已令普通人及國際投資者深感不安。中共的「侵佔三部曲」殖插香港，在「全面管治權」下，所有敵對聲音，近乎已經滅聲。

寫此文時，我人在寶島臺灣，感受到自由民主空氣。美國的CNN在臺灣開始亞洲分社，加拿大的CBC同樣落腳於此。臺灣副總統賴清德正式被民進黨的黨內提名，競逐總統寶座。中國國臺辦再次點名臺灣駐美代表蕭美琴為「臺獨頑固分子」，禁止蕭美琴及其家屬進入中港澳。

上一次的臺灣選舉中，民進黨在九合一選舉大敗，年輕人不出來投票。二〇二四年一月的總統大選，是否會是臺灣的「生死存亡」？在這關鍵時刻，筆者相信臺灣「新世代」會出來投票。前臺灣總統馬英九出訪大陸已回來，可說是劣評如潮；中共何時「真攻臺」，沒有人能夠準確預測。相反的，在香港，這都市繼續玩「人鬥人」，情何以堪。共產黨的宣傳機器，香港人已沒有反抗能力，卻天天「被港獨」；臺灣則天天「被臺獨」。習近平的戰鬥性格，狀態甚勇。世界局勢也緊張，進入準戰爭狀態。

香港已沒兩制，仍講馬照跑？

究竟是北京還是李家超團隊令香港人家散人亡，這點已不重要了；曾經的國際大都市，現在面目全非。夏寶龍剛完結訪港，只准你炒般、跑馬、跳舞、但禁止遊行。極權之下，資金外逃，移居及移民者湧現，香港正在「大換血」。香港人往後可能只是一種「概念」，舊有的香港價值盡失，聽者唏噓。曾經居住過在香港的人，會有自己不同的方法去演繹。

在我而言，世界的香港，本應就是「左中右」聲音也存在，大家可以相信法治，香港仍然是世界金融中心；這一切，自港版國安法實施之後，已經幻滅。港版國安法生效至今，立法會已變了舉手機器，各香港大專院校淪陷；為共產黨賣命的香港代理人繼續要「完善」了各選舉制度後，香港再沒有批判聲音。

鄧小平一九七四年在聯合國的演講曾經這樣說：如果中共變了強大，對外恃強凌弱，那就必須「揭露它，反對它，並且同中國人民一道，打倒它」。再遠些時候，毛澤東在一九四六年曾說：「中國最需要的只是民主……中國人民，緊緊要求如英、法、美及其他民族的人民享有已久的那種權利」。原來頭兩代領導人也知道極權共產行不通。

中國權貴走資的資金超過數萬億美元。毛主席和鄧公已不再，時代也不同，但這兩位強人，雖令中國陷入浩劫，也令那個年代的人瘋狂。誰也應明白到，強權壓下，人民必定反抗。

在香港，根據 Hong Kong Watch 資料顯示，約兩百二十億英鎊現在因 BNO 持有人移居英國，香港的強積金公司不受理贖回。MPF 政治化，拿不下；財金官員許正宇在英國開會，示威者「人肉擋車」可以理解。

習近平管治下的香港，香港其實已再沒有「一國兩制」一‧○模式，這都市已經好像「大監獄」一樣。活在香港「場內監獄」的政治犯，要面對酷熱天氣；活在監獄外的香港人，人身自由和基本人權同樣被奪去。多少人多了政治考量，了解到香港全方位的潛在風險：政治、經濟、個人──活在恐懼中。鐵窗內的生活並不好受，因為失去自由，是真正的痛苦。

此一刻，你還可以說，香港還是香港，應該沒有「秘密刑場」，但精神折磨，在囚與否，港人並不好受。自二○一九年，四年多的抗爭當中，其實香港人的變化，難以用筆墨去形容。

在監獄內，單獨囚禁，是酷刑其中一種；要戰勝恐懼，必須要有思想上的準備。香港全方位邁向大陸化，而在這急速變化的慘痛過程中，在囚或在香港大監獄外，身心及體魄必須作出好的調教，在逆境中求存。香港的一國兩制，確實實驗已失敗。現在還看臺灣，可否堅守下去！

民主遊行已成絕響

港版國安法實施接近了三年時間，泛民及公民社會全面瓦解。五一遊行，前職公民主席黃迺元被帶走，因為個人申請遊行，最近頻密在媒體出現，懷疑被警方「帶走問話」。長話短說，已經撤回五一遊行申請，也因為「宇宙國安大法」所限，無法解釋原因。夏寶龍大叔話齋，遊行不是一定表達訴求的方式，香港從未如此墮落，一句屁話，個個跪低，踐踏基本法給予香港人應有的自由。

除了五一，還有六四、七一這些極權認為是的「敏感時刻」。筆者可以寫包單，只要有「民主表達訴求」成份的遊行，在夏先生到訪後，不經思考的治港者，只會殺雞儆猴，香港「靜音」。在二○一九年前的世界，前人大朱幼麟，前全國政協劉夢熊也會出席泛民搞的遊行，這是思想自由的表達，在宇宙大法下，這也消失了。

鄧炳強保安局長是香港「戰狼的戰狼」，任何事情政治化，這是在新香港下，只會嚇走更多金融及商業機構。新鮮滾熱辣：加拿大安大略省的退休基金《安大略省教師退休基金》Ontario Teachers' Pension Plan, OTPP）也已正式撤出香港，把中國股票投資團隊解散。中國與其

他國家在政治上「升級」，或許進入準戰爭狀態，基金經理便是投資公司最大資產，及早撤離，正路不過。地緣政治極度兇險；而整個香港，不知不覺「被改造」中。建制及藍絲也估不到，香港這樣急促的沉淪。

數十萬港人移居英國，若有一半是「藍絲加建制」，也不出奇。但很可惜，當泛民自回歸前的一九八四年爭取民主，到二○二○年六月三十號國安法實施實施前，太多義人「被犧牲」。中國的劉曉波可算是慘死，維權律師被「重刑」，異見者更可以是「死無葬身」之地。國安案件服刑完結後，多少曾經是「有影響力」的人會被軟禁？這是值得正視的問題。

中共現在「假大空」的強勢，戰狼高調「拆人大臺」，不理會外界的批判聲音，相信不會停。曾幾何時，一撮港人在中聯辦門外示威、靜坐。有宗教團體在中聯辦門外祈禱靜坐，現在也可能變成顛覆國家政權。在政治大棋局下，習權天下，永遠稱帝，形勢已定。

中共下一步會否攻打臺灣？美國共和黨的總統競爭者 Vivek 建議，臺灣每家每戶有槍械，對抗中共。其實在臺灣外島金門等地，接近中國的島嶼，每家每戶每家每戶也有槍械，而非兩千多萬人口的每戶臺灣家庭。我只可說，發生了才算吧，誰可預知？香港人還是關心，最迫切的事情。如果香港人的核心價值只是「有得搵食」，這是很可悲的事情。而現在的港共宣傳機器是要「用心去愛黨」，甚至「為黨犧牲」，將會更多人離開香港。共產黨的一舉一動，確實令世人不安。

致富心態，貪錢作怪

華爾街日報專欄作家 Morgan Housel 在二〇二〇年出版的《致富心態》（The Psychology of Money），講述很多投資行為並非那麼科學化。投資的決定，很多時夾雜了個人情緒、自尊心，環境因素而作出抉擇。而有一句老話形容投資行為以及賺錢途徑都很貼切，即：「心態便是境界」。

至於貪婪，很多時候是萬惡之根，令人脫離了真道。貪錢，是否做人的原動力？一九八〇年代中，有一部膾炙人口的警世電影Wall Street，中文片名為《華爾街》，裡面一句名言：貪婪是好，英文就是 Greed Is Good，把美國紐約的金融中心華爾街為形容金融從業員，一個只向前／錢看的行業。無論是暢銷書或暢銷電影，甚至財經肥皂劇，這類型的題材，永久長青，必有市場。

心戰領域，有炒家曾說，要有近乎破產的經歷才可浴火重生，所以他天天著迷買輪、長短期指、倫敦金等。有位世伯，七十有中，十年來炒金累積輸了一百萬元，因為要有所謂的精神寄託，在這領域追逐日光，真是 too bad so sad。我想在此一提《操盤手回憶錄》一書，可說

是二〇二三年必須一看或重看的「奇書」。書中主角 Jesse Liver more 曾說：「市場只有一個方向，不是作多、不是作空，而是對的方向」。Well，這位上世紀初的一代股神經歷數次破產，最後更吞槍自殺，這又是個很好的破產經驗、或反面教材。

市場有一句名言：Sell In May and Walk Away。還未有「高頻交易」世界的時候，確實在五至八月，這四個月時間，股票成交會比較稀疏。高頻交易早是大勢所趨，「趨勢」並非那麼容易估中，但技巧為本的操作，可說是多的是。市場的賺與蝕，一切其實是過眼雲煙。

大型對沖基金有它們的獲利投資竅門，不會容易話你知。散戶的世界，可行的法則無數，這裡只供參考：一，中長線投資，二，減少槓桿，三，投資上的「心戰」定位要清晰。我對你說，你如果做即日市，大戶的高頻交易好像把時間短線停頓一樣，有壓縮的力量，把獲利機會發揮到淋漓盡致，「事成」後，你獲利機會已減低（因量大的程序「落飛」及「抽出」令交易做到合法性地雜亂），你的速度不只「慢半拍」，而是變成了「慢幾拍」。

最後，在投資的領域，很多是靠一手的江湖經驗，但沒有對與錯。大家要緊記，「攻心為上」。很多時的投資決定，成敗得失來自心態，所以「心態便是境界」。一個人的快樂與否，理應不是從戶口有多少錢，總資產值有多大所影響。我們必須懷著謙卑的心，了解到金錢帶不走，在短暫的人生，「活著」已是充滿著無限可能。我們更要積極面對每一天。

香港噤聲下，人財兩空

一九八九年，六四發生，中共通緝了二十一名學生領袖。王丹、吾爾開希、柴玲及周鋒鎖，代表了他／她們這一代人追求民主的訴求。二〇一九年，香港人也有「時代革命」，犧牲太多，需要沉澱。香港的六四活動已成絕響，高志活藝術家的「國殤之柱」已被國安警「充公」，可能成為何俊仁、李卓人及周幸彤的「加罪」證物。

把話題延伸。筆者暫居海外，到處漂泊；和多倫多大學商學院學生，特別是中國大陸讀商科的學生接觸，想了解他們對六四的看法。三十四年了。六四事件，在中國學生的眼中是否「存在」？說白一點，中國大陸學生，甚至大部份的大陸人，不僅不關注，也樂意接受一個謊言的社會與極權的統治。其實過去幾年，香港同樣發生極大變化。天安門悲劇發生三十多年，中共只鼓吹港人「炒股票、馬照跑、舞照跳」，搵銀至上。香港已經失去靈魂，沒有言論、集會及思想的自由。六四在中共港共治港者的眼中，是一個「禁區」，必須淡化與遺忘。

而中國人當然也明白「自由價更高」。我的黨員「半生熟」之交，很多都是這樣想⋯⋯「錢留在中國，並不是自己的錢。出入自由也不是必然」。

中共權貴將數萬億美元的資產藏匿在世界各地，相當誇張。涉及的不義之財，早已離岸。

這不是小數目，是美國GDP的三分之一，真正的「大茶飯」。文章開始，我們談到八九六四，中共的二十一名通緝犯中，李祿（LiLu，一九六一）排名第十八，他幾經艱辛，一九九〇年代初在美國著名長春藤哥倫比亞大學完成了學士、MBA及法學博士，於一九九七年設立投資公司Himalaya Capital。已成為美國人的李祿，曾與股神巴菲特在二〇一〇年出席比亞迪汽車公司於深圳舉辦的活動，這是他自六四流亡之後首次公開露面。在當時，似乎疑似是巴菲特的接班人，即便是民運學生也不是問題；在中共眼裡，每個人都有個「價」，只是「錢作怪」；但要「返枱」時，你可能喪命，人身安全沒有保障。

再說回香港。如今支聯會的骨幹成員全部在監獄；六四集會已成顛覆國家政權的活動，情何以堪。支聯會前副主席周幸彤最近獲南韓頒發「光州人權獎」，世界仍然關注香港。已故的鄧小平希望香港有不同的聲音，已仙遊的自由黨創黨主席李鵬飛、李柱銘及黎智英，捍衛了香港多年的民主及法治與自由；後者被噤聲入獄，令人心痛。

《港版國安法》現在燒到銀行高端客戶：沒有章法，隨意凍結、充公及拘捕，不但令這曾經的國際金融中心響起警鐘，也意味著香港已不再安全。現在失控的香港，徹底破壞了鄧小平在六四悲劇後，修補世人對中華人民共和國與香港特別行政區的看法。若是香港的超級富豪，現在將擔心隨時在香港人財兩空！

港共表忠，民主國家不可裝睡

看到特首李家超在立法會大談「外部勢力惡意破壞香港未有減退」，實在令人悲痛。慘不忍睹之處，在於現時香港的「治港者」不斷標榜香港有很大的外部勢力破壞，無中生有，製造假想敵；不稱職的人當官，決定了香港的命運。

立法會的行政長官「互動交流會」變成「表忠大會」。李慧琼算是香港人認識的名字，做了她的一分鐘「擦鞋騷」；又有位叫陳勇的議員，代表中國人大政協及中國全國性團體代表界，不熟悉的界別，陌生的面孔，臺上發言有等於冇，立法會成為橡皮圖章。

九十位立法會議員，有一名所謂的「反對派」叫狄志遠，關心政治的不會陌生，當然問了也等於冇問。假如你是做官，你只要說香港有「港獨問題」隨時引爆，需要處理。吹得香港保安問題那麼大，你又過一關，政府官員由上而下，「本科」的實事又不再需要處理了。這就是現今的香港故事，曾經的技術性官員，現在買少見少。香港建制派現在控制香港命脈，多少個只是「呃飯食」，大家心照。

至於區議會，選舉產生方法關卡重重，基本上是愛國者才可以入閘。資深區議員，前公民

黨的司馬文，切切實實說到，今屆完結後，不會競逐參選。參選與否，筆者沒有太大的意見，但「優化」了之後的假選舉，其實是幫助政權「抬橋」，去馬與否，畫公仔不需要畫出腸吧，你明的。

臺灣總統選舉在二〇二四年一月舉行，過去數月，郭台銘決定「讓位」，叫他的粉絲支持新北市市長侯友宜。看侯的資料作盡職審查，現在開始變得「有趣」。他是紀律部隊出身。如無意外，民進黨推出的賴清德，對外交事務經驗高出幾班。

過去兩屆臺灣總統大選，筆者曾到臺灣觀戰。香港已經沒有民主選舉，去臺灣「取經」意義不大。代表國民黨的侯友宜反對臺獨，也不信任中共的「一國兩制」；至於賴清德副總統，認為世界已經默認臺灣是主權國家，什麼「臺獨」命題，重要嗎？

二〇二三年的中共，處於戰狼「強勢」，手法及言語行為極為強硬，但執行時更「乾淨」，可以有秘密警察在海外把你「送中」，可以干預外國選舉結果，共產黨就是「食住你」，民主國家，不可能也不可以再裝睡。

一年已巨變，何況已三年？

在「靜音」後的香港，講句話都要「諗過度過」。白色恐怖下，隨時犯國安法，這不是很好的香港故事，但暫時無法改變。二〇一九前的世界，香港人勇敢反抗，爭取民主與自由。港版國安法實施後，逮捕、禁錮，也能「出師有名」，歪理當真理。

政治評論，香港人心灰意冷。中國大陸棟篤笑講員，是否把解放軍「開玩笑」？又拉又鎖兼罰錢，這是政治現實。外國版有馬來西亞裔、現居英國的網上食評家兼笑口騷演員 Uncle Roger，對中共政權、評級及華為監控開玩笑，結果微博帳戶立刻被封。假如 Uncle Roger 在中國開騷，可能淪為加拿大的兩個 Michaels，最後與華為公主孟晚舟互相「交換人質」。

二〇二三年，一項原本很有意義的器官捐贈計劃，卻因為沒有諮詢的「共享互通」計劃，讓港人對特區政府信心動搖。幾名立法會議員再提「假設默許」Silent Consent，如果你無 check mark 不願意捐贈，你的「人體器官」可能變相受惠於中國內地同胞。資料顯示，有三十幾萬登記「捐贈器官」的香港人，這比率遠高於中國內地人。自二〇二三年十二月到二〇二三年四月，政府鬼鼠加插與中國內地「共享互通」，香港人強烈地有反應。自己的器官死後如何處

理，正常社會下，當然取決於個人自由意志。李家超「軍管」特首的破壞力驚人，智商更加嚇人，又話要警方加入調查，荒謬絕倫。

數年前香港的「一地兩檢」爭議，和今天的人體器官「共享互通」操作上極為相似，值得我們重溫。「一地兩檢」未經諮詢強加推行，令港人反感；與二〇〇三年強推《基本法》二十三條無異，也是變相在香港實施大陸法，香港人怎可不警惕？中國借西九，一借無回頭。《基本法》十八條列明，香港除國防以及外交外，不可實行大陸法律，通關及出入境等屬香港自治範圍，而西九高鐵站實行「割地兩檢」並非純法律問題，也有不少灰色地帶，將引發更多社會問題。

當年金融界的朋友問，國安公安捉你我去「租界」，香港警察會否阻止？跨境學童殺到九龍，淪陷地區可能包括九龍塘、何文田等名校區，交通上有潛在的大混亂風險。高鐵到二〇四七難回本，蝕了幾多億，還是無底深潭？就如高鐵的「無極限」超支，無人能準確解答。

港版國安法實施近三年，香港已沒有真正的「兩制」，大陸法正在香港實施中。無論你是什麼「顏色」都能感受到，香港距離一個正常運作的城市，已經天差地遠。

走筆之時，國泰三名服務員疑似因對中國大陸的乘客「講英文」而被解僱，這是一間公司沉淪的延續篇。國泰航空，原本建基於香港。香港人講廣東話及英文，這是他的「本能」。機

上服務員講國語「唔鹹唔淡」，詞不達意，可能更糟糕。講「中國國語」大晒，當然㗎到香港，大陸人話香港人「冇禮貌」。國泰用高壓「處理」事件，再加上「陀槍」的李家超為國際事件說三道四，又干他何事？一年已巨變，何況這個宇宙惡法，已實施接近三年？唯有說聲：香港人加油。

港股變天，勇氣不滅

港股低處未算低。美國三大指數，反覆徘徊。以科技股為主打的納斯達克指數、道瓊斯及標準普爾500，二○二三年三月份曾經坐「過山車」。芝加哥期權波動指數 VIX，現時在十七・九四左右徘徊當中。強勢主力股如蘋果（AAPL），現市值大約為二・七萬億美元。微軟公司（MSFT）現時市值約為二・四萬億美元。在香港的永久居民投資美股時，沒有資本增值稅，只有股息收入稅，理論上是「賺盡」。

當然，馬照跑、舞照跳、股照炒的槓桿投機者，也有過輸到「褲穿窿」的狀態。香港現在時局不同，曾經的國際金融城市，又變為由一個不受監管的無形之手「高度操控」。所有留下的大中小型商業機構，也會重新評估政治風險，因為在各領域已近乎等同於中國大陸，大家再也不能裝睡。

有操盤新人王問：乜嘢係「最好炒的股票」？對於短線炒賣的操作者，可能是大銀碼、成交量高、每天有波動的股票。每天只有數十萬、不足一百萬成交量的股票，則應盡量避免。「Thinly traded stocks」不是很多人的「那杯茶」，差價 bid-ask spread 太闊，很多時候容易中伏。

這關乎什麼市場，主打每天有絕對回報的坐盤交易員，除了主力長短倉作組合的建倉根基，也會考慮加入對沖策略，如期權及期貨。波動產品 VIX 有期貨、期權及 VIX 的 ETF。條條大路通羅馬，務求達致絕對回報。

中共除非滅了所有舊香港人，繼續「淡化」六四事件，令十三億人口矇在鼓裡；但我心底深處更相信，雖然現在香港已經「噤聲」，維園燭光不再，香港人依然有的是「正義感及良知」，這是金錢不容易買到的東西，六四精神不會容易熄滅。

還有，世界香港論壇涉及的範疇，包括宗教、政治、投資及文化傳承。二〇二三年九月便將在加拿大舉行，希望大家有所啟迪。

最後，善用香港最後價值，捍衛法治、自由，真理及良知，聽落好大路，多元化投資於一些「有形」及「無形」的東西，理性面對新的形勢，特別是兇猛的政治形勢，這是刻不容緩的。莫認為現在的狀態是正常的。香港人加油。

高機率投資，尋獲利之道

事先聲明，「高機率」也可能輸到一敗塗地。任何投資，順勢而行是大原則。在ＨＦＴ高頻交易前的世界，交易員用五至八月這四個月份，相對可以「預測」市場走勢，現在千祈唔好「估市」走勢。美國循序漸進入加息周期的「尾聲」，大市波動是必然。

MAANG+ 股票組合，代表 Meta、前身叫 Facebook、Amazon、Apple、Netflix及Alphabet，即 Google 母公司。串流娛樂技術公司 Netflix 用戶的選擇多了，自家製作的劇集，特別是動作片，近期越戰越勇。Netflix 找了前加州州長，阿諾史瓦辛格作 Netflix（NFLX）的動作片執行官（Chief Action Officer），絕對是不二之選，多了吸客理由。

科技股歷史高位反覆，Meta 股價更是慘不忍睹。MAANG+股票汰弱留強，正常不過。正股昂貴，投機者又不希望有風險地做期權 Call，審慎樂觀的策略，當然有牛市認購跨價買賣策略 Bull Call Debit Spread。做 Spread，你的期權付出溢價相對減低。另一邊廂，固定波動策略離不開這些動作：購入正股，在高行駛價做 write call，在低行使價 long put，這是持了倉，更想護盤的方法。到最後，每個投資部位都要計算精準，作高機率投資（High probability trade）。

美國和中國博弈，中美因貿易及臺灣問題，隨時可以「反枱」。但走到最深處，畢竟問題在於雙方核心價值不同。從政治經濟博弈來看，美國本土在二〇二三年也進入關鍵時刻，因為共和黨有「初選」。前總統川普及現任總統拜登，二〇二四年底是否會面對面「再戰」，這是很多人關注的事情。前副總統彭斯有參選意向，前國務卿龐貝奧講明不會參選，支持任何一位共和黨友，他的「祝福」絕對有幫助，但並非具最大影響力。香港人可能對龐貝奧有太大的期望，卻沒有實質的效果。

Netflix 用戶每月支付幾十元港幣，絕對是不錯的娛樂。鐵拳俠 Man With the Iron Fist 是一年多前被吹捧的 Netflix 劇集，與漫畫英雄鐵拳俠兼億萬富豪主角一起對付邪惡的 Madam Gau，是懂得控制人類思想的中國黑幫女強人，娛樂指數甚高。劇集加入亞洲元素，當然是因為亞太區的龐大市場，劇集一於「汁都撈埋」。Sell The World 模式源自上世紀九〇年代末的互聯網熱潮，現在內容就是王。就像加入甄子丹去做 John Wick 殺神電影的最大奸角，完全為了市場需要。

二〇二三年上半年邁入尾聲，我也很留意迪士尼（DIS）夏季和秋季的股票表現情況，經濟永遠可以更好，依然會有很多人願意消費。

世界的香港，最後守護者

香港國安法官的「蝦碌」事件已成為國際新聞，還上了 BBC，唔俾佢嚇死，都俾佢笑死。香港國安法官被揭發判詞屬「司法抄襲」，即百分之九十八判詞，照版 copy and paste，技術性叫 judicial copying。這位國安法官名叫陳嘉信，是審理《願榮光歸香港》是否會成為「禁歌」的主理人；而此案件現改為 7.21 號高等法院審理。香港政府還未找到《榮光》禁制令抗辯者，即暫無指定的人或機構「接招」，究竟告哪位？

由於陳嘉信法官已被首席大法官張舉能「嚴厲訓示」，《榮光》案被換人審理，也絕對有可能。執筆時，蘋果 iTunes 及 Apple Music 已把《願榮光歸香港》在香港及海外近乎全面下架。另一邊廂，則反而有不少世界各地的廣播電臺，因港府的「禁播令」而受激發，播放起《願榮光歸香港》。經香港政府「推特」，人類歷史上可能會有首宗全球禁制令嗎？正常情理下，並不可能。

中共港共不喜歡人民思考，只要你人照跑、舞照跳以及股票照炒，這可能是香港人的輪迴宿命。我預計七一遊行和六四集會一樣，只會是香港人的歷史，是記憶禁區。住在香港的港

人，現在所追尋的，究竟是什麼？經過了二〇一九年社會事件後，可能「左中右」最大的公約數，便是做低頭族，埋頭苦幹，不問世事，繼續賺錢？這其實是很可悲的事情。如果香港的稅制能有所改變，那麼例如股票，便應當設定「資本增值」稅，股息收入同樣如是。否則香港對小投資者而言，已沒有相對的優勢。

財富累積，理論上是在三十至四十年間，當有賺錢能力時，把資金投進資本市場，用更進取的投資策略，累積財富。香港恒生指數由歷史上最高的三萬多點，到現在的萬九點徘徊，反映了股票市場市值回吐；這也和上證綜合指數的回調相輔相成。相對於「低壓力」的投資組合，一般人會選擇善用指數基金ETF，放在資本市場上。美國標普500指數的SPY、道瓊斯指數的DOW能分散風險。然而，市場必然有波動，在中長線投資，即一般人所說的三年或以上，會製造無限可能。

時移勢易，香港投資及政治環境，越來越嚇人。高端客戶也會注意到要在政治不穩定的情況下，把辛苦賺來的資金放在離岸帳戶。風險投資，即作任何的risk taking，坦白說也是「順其自然」，絕對無需強求。二〇〇八年雷曼兄弟倒閉，多少對沖基金出事；過去數年，另一「出事」的資產類別則是加密貨幣。投資除了操作技巧之外，大家更要關注「對家風險」，即counter party risk。

香港的真價值，其實就是和中國內地不同。香港最值錢的地方，並非只是金融及地產，管治班子的好與壞，能夠令世界「有信心」，這同樣重要。香港現在太多「擦鞋黨」湧現，情況不理想。「愛國心」需要隨心而發，從來也不應是「責任」。現在香港也進入「文字獄」的大時代，這和「說好香港故事」成了強烈對比。

香港的最後戰場，不只在香港的地域界限內，而是在世界的香港。海外的香港人將會越來越多，他們也有責任說好香港故事。香港人的角色不斷在轉變，不能只沉溺於「舊香港」的世界，緬懷 good old days。當四十七人案、蘋果案及支聯會的「終極審判」完結後，我們又如何行落去？香港人當不斷努力，令世界再次認受「香港價值」為何物，我們便是香港最後的守護者。

香港有燶味，這個夏天螞蟻搬家

香港各種大小的「維護國家安全」案件繼續開審。「靜音之下」，各人心情沉重。加息周期持續，借貸周轉成本增加，應否繼續，主導權在自己。在政治行先的香港，任何事情風險大增。香港人去或留成為主體，說好香港故事，難上加難。我的自家 YouTube 頻道 @EdChinWorld，閒時會做一些碌街節目，經過中環，食肆不停地轉。雲咸街、威靈頓街、當然還有蘭桂坊，歷經新冠疫情三年多的「洗禮」後，政權也留意到，舊香港人如果再沒有「為香港出力」之心，這一代人，需要更換。

說好香港故事，不如先做好香港故事。強權壓下，我的建制「半生熟」之交，同樣早已發覺「燶味」，今次是香港的資金轉移及人口轉移。港元兌美元，沽港幣揸美金仍然一面倒，利率上升再加上中國經濟增長放緩，香港的大行情，絕對不妙，對地產大行情，更加不妙。黎智英案預計將在二○二三年九月尾開審；在四十七人案的持久審訊過程中，一些支持者也感到疲倦。一位資深抗爭者這樣對我說：Hong Kong Can Wait。一場公義之戰，是持久的。縱然現在泰山壓頂，無論是何立場：講真話、憑公義、好憐憫，這是我們做人應有的本分。

如今，建制「擦鞋黨」大權在握，香港的監察已經脆弱不堪。我的藍絲「半山熟」之交，已於二〇二三年夏天展開有組織、有預謀的「螞蟻搬家」，每日在環球金融系統轉錢去加拿大。每日上限：一百萬港幣。再說一次，我的建制半山熟之交，聞到香港有「燶味」，像森林的野獸，逃跑到另外一處。

執筆之時，正逢端午。筆者對於龍舟水，沒有太大的漣漪。屈原曾經是楚國大臣，因為小人當道，最終投江自盡。現代人繼續扒龍舟、包粽子來紀念屈原，亦成為端午節的習俗；套用到現今的香港，因香港的「變」，你會否因此而「自盡」？當然不會，挺身發憤圖強，繼續闖蕩，將會更勝舊家鄉。

一國兩制的下半場已近一年，港人到處漂泊，建立「新香港」。已故的黃霑有首歌詞：鄧小平 is coming to town。這是寫在六四屠城之後不久的歌詞。如果可以返回兩制，香港才有望復原。再講多次，現在的寒蟬效應，多了許多「加速師」，只會加速毀滅香港，這曾經的國際都市已正在經歷前所未有的慘況。

香港曾是強力品牌

　　香港曾經是福地，造就了無數奇蹟。整體而言，香港曾經也是「強力品牌」。二○二○年中後，一切也改變。根據一份研究報告，現今的香港，「堅定不移」留下來的人佔了三成人口；但七成人想離開、準備離開，或者已經離開，這極不尋常。極權管治下，溫水煮蛙式的謊言在威權下再也不需遮遮掩掩了，外國投資者嚇怕。新加坡接收了不少香港的專才，五眼聯盟國家，特別是英國及加拿大，加速了「搶人才」的遊戲。香港若特赦黎智英、戴耀廷及黃之鋒等人，曾經的經濟奇蹟，過往的強力品牌，必然可以「翻身」。

　　另一天空下，強力品牌並非一定永遠強勢。美國強力品牌哈利大衛遜（Harley Davidson，代號 HOG）除了是上市公司，大馬力的電單車是發燒友的摯愛，也代表了一種生活態度。我曾經也是哈利發燒友，也會特別留意其他強力品牌有沒有「再戰江湖」之意。多少個電單車牌子過去數十年間 come and go⋯哈利成立於一九○三年，而比哈利還早兩年成立的印地安（Indian Motorcycle）始於一九○一年，又是另一個另類的美國故事。

　　印地安這強力品牌經歷不少風浪。英國電影名星、《沉默的羔羊》電影中的變態教授安東

尼・霍普金斯也為這強力品牌拍了一部電影名為《超速先生》（The fastest Indian），戲中的主角以六十二歲高齡駕駛全世界最快的印地安，打破了當時電單車最快速度。印地安是一九一〇年全球最大的電單車製造廠，在二次大戰期間成為美軍重要的軍用電單車。信不信由你，印地安也曾被國際車壇譽為最經典的摩托車，但到了一九五三年印地安經歷破產風波，隨之消沉。

不知是否電影效應，這部二〇〇五年出品的《超速先生》，講到美國史上第二大電單車強力品牌的盛世與衰落。幾番轉折，以美國明尼蘇達州為基地的戶外活動及越野車集團「美國北極星集團」（Polaris Group，代號 PII），最終在二〇一一年收購了印地安，令這百年經典生命得以延續。

哈利的機構性投資者比重占了百分之九十，ROE 為百分之二十九．；而印地安母公司北極星的機構性投資者比重則為百分之九十二．五，ROE 則為百分之五十六．一四。母公司北極星有多元化的雪地及非公路行駛的田園車輛出產，投資上北極星似乎收入來源更多，而印地安的無限復活如果真的再紅爆，哈利的一哥巡航車地位必然受到威脅。

強力品牌很多時候會經歷經濟上的盛衰循環。上市公司的買賣，情勢不對便可以「冷血」地止血，把它活賣掉。一個地區，一個國家，由盛轉衰，人也要作出抉擇。香港已變，這也是不爭的事實。加拿大剛剛推出「無極限」的 Stream B 救生艇計劃，真的是「搶人才」。再沒有

學歷要求，只要能在當地「繼足分數」工作一年，即可申請永久居住，變為加拿大人。作為人，就是應該永遠有「選擇權」。祝大家好運！

香港笑不出，七一好安靜

二〇二三年，俄羅斯傭兵瓦格納集團首腦普里格津的二十四小時「兵變」，喚醒了很多香港人，認為自身在極權下的處境與其甚為相似。獨裁者的最後收場是：瓦格　首腦稱沒有手下過檔（跳槽）作俄羅斯正規軍，瓦格納雜牌軍到了白俄，實際上是開了第二條入侵烏克蘭的戰線，左右夾攻烏克蘭。一時之間，普京的下場難料，習近平會否「右上限」支持普京，拭目以待。

至於現下的香港，假想敵特別多。居然行政長官和保安局長講到香港「好危險」似，究竟誰在借題發揮，把香港變作一個「靜音下的香港」，大家心照。五眼聯盟當中，美國佬最值，知道香港的「一國兩制」慘不成形，這是鐵一般的事實，不需要解釋的。就算六四、七一，也已是歷史，依正常人的指標，就是當香港沒有政治犯，六四及七一可有遊行表達訴求，香港才能有機會「翻身」。

筆者和劉夢熊先生是「一國兩制」的少數「最後捍衛者」。我指的捍衛，是返回二〇一九年前的「兩制」世界，容納不同的批判聲音。現在治港者「一尾靠嚇」，這更加打擊香港，這

是「軍管」政府不會明白的事情。其實不論誰當特區政府首長，只要違背自由市場、言論自由、思想自由、結社自由、獨立司法這些大原則，香港都只會越來越差。筆者也相信，政權如果心虛，香港必然在競爭力先完結，後倒塌。

說到香港金融。匯豐，香港人熟悉的銀行。他們的頭版廣告有一年是這樣寫的：「環球金融，地方智慧」，簡淺易明。匯豐的問題跟其他銀行一樣，同樣是監管問題。二〇一二年，匯豐因為沒有遵守反洗錢法，為伊朗組織「漂白」黑錢，被美國政府罰款十九.二億美元，這算是相對高額的罰款。投資銀行高盛在二〇〇八年金融海嘯下，售賣不少結構性產品，與抵押債務證券 CDS 有關，同樣被美國政府重罰，監管機構沒有「大細超」（大小眼）。

二〇二三年下半年，首先應關注匯豐三件事：一，匯豐自二〇二三年七月十六號起，便不能從香港環球系統轉賬到加拿大的匯豐第三方帳戶。二，社民連被匯豐關掉戶口，已接觸環球行政總裁 Noel Quinn。三，匯豐Expat離岸帳戶測試特別待遇「不活躍」dormant account的處理手法，如何再次「激活」戶口。

香港投資者，同樣對匯豐又愛又恨。這是一隻表現甚差的股票。雖然高息率（Divid end Yield），但股價不斷重創，也某種程度上反映需要「瘦身」。話雖如此，投資永遠涉及風險，股價永遠有上落，今天我們更關注的，是匯豐，特別是香港匯豐，有黨委在幕後作「操盤

人」，是否「跟黨走」引人關注。

香港的「最後政黨」社民連便收到通知，匯豐不會再做他們生意。社民連在銀行的帳戶金額是可以提領出來的，但「不做客戶生意」，這是難以理解的事情。社民連去信英國，找匯豐行政總裁 Noel Quinn 解釋，我盼望見到匯豐的回覆，不能再「推三推四」。我為此一「被封戶口」事件拍了一支影片在自家 youtube 頻道 @EdChinWorld 分析，沒想到七日內便有超過十八萬人次的瀏覽量。我仍然相信，香港人仍深信公義會再降臨香港。回歸二十六年，很悲痛看見香港已「靜音」。

大灣區香港人

根據無線新聞及香港01報導，廣東省政府希望三年內能推動「粵港澳」三地通：護照、證件、業務、數據等。當三地居民統一身份認證，不知下一步，會否「三地身份證也會完全相同」、唯一分別只是身份證上發證地點（即 place of issue）的不同？在「宇宙大法」實施下的香港，曾經的自由城市，還會剩下多少？

如果粵港澳三地真的「成功融合」，那麼香港樓價、工資甚至聯繫匯率會否被人民幣取代？這些議題，必須預早作「對沖」關注。香港人最關注的，必然是個人自由及思想自由。過去這三年，這些也消失了，資產會否有保障，便是更大的議題。二〇二三年舉辦的 APEC，拜登總統和習近平不知「秘談」中是否談及「香港及中國政治犯」的特赦？香港的名單上，有黎智英、黃之鋒及鄒幸彤。

實質上，香港將會全面變成「大灣區‧香港」，這是大時代的慘痛經歷。「一國兩制」，原出自西藏與中國共產黨簽署的《十七條協議》。一九四九年共產黨取得中國政權後，已逐步入侵西藏；一九五一年的藏中《十七條協議》，其實是中國共產黨要藏人「硬食」；至一九五

九年後變成一百二十萬西藏人被中國共產黨滅族式的血腥鎮壓。中共也吞併了約四分之一所謂屬於「中國版圖」的疆域。先「佔領」、後屠殺的反人類惡行，層出不窮。西藏的「佔領三部曲」如下：進入西藏、立足西藏、改造西藏。

同樣地，香港經歷二〇一九年的反修例運動，在二〇二〇年中港版國安法實施後，一切已難返回真正的「一國兩制」模式。下筆此刻，筆者剛收到一位港交所前高層朋友，已順利離開香港，在政治壓力下赴英國定居。畢竟，香港已不安全。多少在「宇宙大法」實施後被扣押的香港人，已經超過兩年痛失自由。也有更瘋狂的事情在二〇二三年發生：探監反被拘捕、被還柙扣留；入境因香港強積金贖回的爭議而「被拘捕」，如今這也算是香港的「特點」了。那麼，如何真的可以唱好香港故事？

陳茂波因 APEC 和習近平「咬耳仔」可能風騷片刻，回到香港後，特區團隊為了「坐穩」繼續互相廝殺。在李家超管治下，白色恐怖假不了。雖然外資行不會成為「絕響」，但香港作為一等一的國際金融城市，已然是「過去式」。五十年不變的神話已經幻滅，大家不妨多點想像空間，如何建立「世界的香港」。

香港並非無藥可救

香港大大小小的終極審判，正在進行中。二〇二三年七月底前，四十七人案到了前立場姐姐何桂藍作供。阿藍二〇一九年在元朗七二一的報導確實專業，也被白衣人打到周身傷痕。對她的審訊與其他人一樣，獻上無限祝福。此刻，我也想念在獄中的毛孟靜及鄒幸彤，他們為香港已付出了一切，是罕見的女中豪傑。

現今的香港其實正在經歷現代版文革。金融世界講求利益，一些扮成「好愛國」的半生熟之交，憑著關係賺了一些錢，九至十位數字身家的，來到接近退休年紀，更希望安享晚年。時移勢易，在「新香港」制度下，建制的半生熟朋友，大多數搞移民或回流，繼續表面愛國；但他們更明白，香港沒有所謂的反對黨，沒有批判聲音，他們更加腳軟。

我相信鄧小平原先構思的一國兩制，並非要香港人「疑神疑鬼」，安全欠奉。相信當時他也明白八九六四屠城後，改革開放必然會引入國際社會認同的價值觀、法治、人權及自由。鄧小平差點便可見證九七回歸，結果早幾個月前離世。若要實現一國兩制的偉大構思，就是要有真正的三權分立，真正的港人治港，不是京人治港，而這一切在二〇二〇年七月後已經幻滅。

有位半生熟之交對我說：鄧小平已「死咗好耐」，你覺得共產黨講嘅嘢會係真的嗎？你們玩斯文，還信香港有法治，可能真的是很天真很傻。已故中國全國政協副主席安子介曾說：「港人治港最重要的是港法治港」。一國兩制下半場的說法已沒有新意思，香港人已到處漂泊，建立「新香港」。現在的寒蟬效應，港版國安法做了「加速師」，這曾經的國際都市，也正在經歷前所未有的慘痛狀況！

最後，香港真的回到文革時代，什麼「軟對抗」的笑話也說得出。香港不能變成極端的左，就正如中國大陸的政治ＫＯＬ靖海侯也警告，香港的治港者不要什麼都「國安法」，如此濫用絕對令香港走向不歸路。在我而言，返回鄧小平一．〇版本的「一國兩制」才是正路。還有，特赦所有政治犯，是其中一個選項，因為一九七七年麥理浩爵士也曾經特赦香港貪污警察，這是政治動作，為何不可？

香港迎接各種波動

香港確實有很多問題，最重要的是政治問題無法解決。太多的恐怖故事在新香港不斷發生。八名為了民主奮鬥、為了自由犧牲了自己的香港人變成「國際通緝犯」。如果一國兩制真的在香港存在，一人一票選特首，這些「通緝犯」可以為香港創造更大的未來。但是一國兩制走樣變形，淪為世界笑話；離開，便是走最遠的路。

法律這座大山，說要司法改革，由年前說要除去法官的「假髮」做起，亦提出要廢除大律師的稱銜，亦即讓香港更像中國大陸。香港其實已只剩「半條命」，也變成完全行heartbeat，政權玩緊大換血，非比尋常。「立場姐姐」在四十七人案當中，答辯精準（內容請看《法庭線》等媒體，有詳盡報導）。唯一要提的，就是何桂藍也明白，在這種畸形的審訊下，答錯些少，可以終身監禁。

在操盤領域，世上沒有完美組合。認識一位專業人士。把酒乾杯後，他說他的避險投資模式是現金、金條及虛擬「貨幣」比特幣。在現金領域，他的港元也不持有太多，差不多全是美金；至於比特幣投資，我本人難以理解；「創辦人」聽說是日本人，但存在虛擬世界。

在我而言，優質主力股的有效策略是用主力股作對沖（Collar，領口策略）、現金（港元或美金），而精選強力品牌公司則需要一生鑽研。結構性產品並非一般人的「那杯茶」，在這引伸波動性（IV）偏高的日子，沾上渦輪、牛熊證等工具不利，除非你每次都「神準」，有能力看透爆起或爆跌。

讓我講一個實戰小故事。我的臺北交易員朋友老陳，沒有家世背景，算是自行坐盤的投資操盤人，他把有限的資金，利用金融槓桿特性，滾大至三十球美金，轉型投資不動產。此外，二〇一七年，股票市場大升，互聯網平台亞馬遜創辦人 Jeff Bezos 因自家公司的股票水漲船高，身家不定期超越比爾蓋茨而成為世界首富，舉世驚訝。香港難有下一個李嘉誠，但什麼才算富有？我相信是各方面的自由。在中國內地，不勞而得之財通常沒有好下場。在科技世界，虛擬貨幣有點兒似富貴浮雲。我還未見到用比特幣可以買得到誠哥的千萬「劏房豪宅」。大泡沫投資，一切如幻影。香港人無力感太重，致富不宜走捷徑。

最後，要尊重市場定律，止蝕（停損）時要超級「冷血」。留意投資機會，但不要把 big bets 變成了 wrong bets。Happy trading.

一國兩制，一切幻影

鄧小平「一錘定音」的一國兩制，走樣變質可說慘不忍睹。日前我與前中國政協劉夢熊一起在網上互動，談到香港未來會變成怎樣。結論是，似乎對現在的處境也只能輕鬆帶過，要「哽住先」。

還要說點「想當年」。在沒有藍黃之分、二〇一四年雨傘運動前的香港，戴耀廷教授發起和平佔中，某種程度上是要向強權暴政說不，也希望當時中共執政近七十年，治國手段會變得文明。筆者過去數年深度研究一九五一年藏中《十七條協議》及港人沒有發言權的一九八四《中英聯合聲明》；時間及處境不同，中藏及中港本應是有原則性的處理，我們卻在歷史中看到實際上淪為統戰、離間、鎮壓，以及「被消失」。

如今來到二〇二三年。香港正在「解放」中。毀了香港的一切，這對中國共產黨就有什麼好處？港人治港，高度自治，本應可以發生；海外港人討論「香港議會」，已經被中共政權說這絕對違反國安法。現在的香港人，到處漂泊，情況不妙。

加拿大總理杜魯多在中國的花名叫做「小土豆」，二〇二三年九月的G20峰會當中，習

近平向小土豆訓話，花生指數（案：吃花生看戲之意）極高。十三億人口，中共當然會有不同方法對抗「邪惡」的西方世界。小土豆是否太天真太傻，還是自己也是利益輸送下的受惠者，他自己才可解答這問題。

加拿大在各級政府選舉當中，被戰狼團隊滲入，宛如中共的「附屬國」。小土豆其實也不能詐傻扮懵，令加拿大國民矇在鼓裡。舉例來說，亞伯特省有中共士兵接受加拿大軍人的山區作戰，這成何體統？

什麼事情，最終還看政治。我認為香港獨立「近乎不可能」，除非香港淪落到每一份政府主要職位、公職都要「上面」祝福，或香港人已經反智到任何事情也作自我審查，人民不顧命地反抗。現在香港的大環境，什麼事情都要背靠祖國，也被活在監控之中。

至於中國內部，北京周邊水災，各級政府處理災情的狼狽情況令人「嘆為觀止」；內地維權律師被查扣打壓；劉曉波遺孀劉霞在媒體上苦泣的畫面不再，因為她已在德國找到自由。二〇二三年邁向最後四個月，港人更加關注農曆新年前的花紅有多少，和同事聊聊北海道滑雪或美加澳紐兩周的假期之旅云云。香港人，不再多談「政治」。

最後，知道譚文豪前議員有份作股東的「一日三餐」餐廳，將在二〇二三年九月底結束營業。業主加租，食物成本增加，更多人移民，難以「對沖」市場正宗。譚也被扣押兩年了，

為了自由民主，犧牲了很多。在「美麗新香港」下，人們還是必須沉著面對，盡量尋找生存空間。

獄中贈畫，人間有情

最近媒體拍到壹傳媒創辦人黎智英先生在赤柱監獄獨自「放風」的圖片，七十五歲的他，也清減了很多。藉此希望隨心而發，寫一些黎先生的舊事。我第一次與黎先生見面，是一九九一年。當年香港還未回歸，筆者正在籌備一九九二年以財經及金融為主打的加拿大多倫多 CHIN Radio 中文廣播。當時還未有蘋果日報，壹週刊已破格而出，也是很多加拿大華人喜歡的刊物。黎生當年魄力驚人；四十三歲的他，對傳媒有著一番熱誠，紡織及零售事業卻正在準備全身而退。第一次見面，很記得 Jimmy 穿了一雙黑色功夫鞋，說話飛快，幹勁十足。

時光飛逝，筆者二千年回流香江，專注於金融及對沖基金事業。再次有機會坐下來與黎生面對面深度傾談，便是在二〇一四年的雨傘運動期間；黎生也算是走在最前線。我心想，他為香港的民主自由，可能會付出一切。黎除了是傳媒人，他過去數十年給筆者的感覺，是真正愛香港、堅持有民主中國的「真香港人」。

二〇一三至二〇一四年，戴耀廷教授發起「和平佔中」。二〇一四年六月，有一天傍晚，筆者代邀請了前政務司陳方安生女士在 I-Cable 的 Money Cafe 作嘉賓；同一天晚上，租了電車數

小時，在香港島宣傳六月二十二日的投票。黎智英、李柱銘、陳方安生、戴耀廷教授在中環雪廠街啟動「真普選 6.22 模擬投票」。當時感覺，香港會有民主的一天。我們眾人舉起蠟燭，象徵了香港終有一天會有民主。

直到二〇一九年的反送中運動，黎生的壹傳媒集團成了政權打壓的對象。國安法實施後，壹傳媒倒下了；到現在兩百多名「國安犯」衍生了，被長期扣留或在保釋當中。黎生是政權的「頭號敵人」，在獄中已被監禁三年；漫長的審訊將會展開，而被判刑後，有可能終身監禁，也有可能死在獄中。言論自由，本應就是香港的基石，現在失去了，香港不再安全。

時光又快閃到二〇二二年底，蘋果前專欄作家李怡先生，在卡加利舉行葬禮。李怡前輩的家人分享了黎生在獄中繪畫「基督釘十字架」的圖畫。李怡比黎生年長十二歲，當時李怡的身體出了毛病，已在監獄「被滅聲」的黎生，送給李怡素描繪畫為他打氣。黎生在赤柱監獄，每天活在「基督的愛與受苦精神」當中。

黎生及蘋果日報的國安案件，原定二〇二三年九月底進行，現在又延期。國安案百分之百入罪，情況並不樂觀，但我仍然相信會有奇蹟，心仍存盼望。多謝你創辦了壹傳媒、壹週刊及蘋果日報雖然已不再，但這數十年的文字及聲音廣播，更令香港人明白，言論自由是香港的基石。我們也要繼續努力，好好地活下去。

香港被清洗，政敵被死亡

二〇二三年八月，俄羅斯的僱傭兵「瓦格納集團」領導人普里格津墜機身亡。俄國官方證實普里格津搭乘的一架私人飛機在半途墜毀，包括他在內，機上十人全數罹難。不少人認為，瓦格納主腦的命運，猶如中共元老、毛澤東時代的左右手林彪，因功高震主，在蒙古境內墜機身亡。普里格津的「被死亡」，在下筆此刻，熱烈被討論。

與此同時，當我們繼續關注四十七人案、蘋果日報案及支聯會案之際，理大學生呂世瑜案，在終院國安法法官（並沒有海外非常任法官）一致駁回呂的上訴，裁定根據《國安法》第二十一條煽動分裂國家罪，判處嚴重罪行，刑期五年以上。就算被告呂世瑜認罪扣減三分之一刑期，亦不能低於最少五年監禁。這算是香港國安法的「底線」，是以五年量刑為起點。

想不到，香港自二〇一九年反修例運動到現在，極速變化，令人陌生。政府最近講到「刺激夜市」，著名的國際會計師事務所 PwC 也質疑政府的做法。中國前全國政協何柱國在電臺節目轟爆現時特區政府的各種做法，認為搞夜市尤如「發春夢」；而另一位中國前全國政協劉夢熊在香港民主黨劉慧卿的節目談到，李家超必須「做好香港故事」，不是吹吹水而已，對於香

港前景，大家心裡有數。

香港現正進入「清洗太平地」時代。八名香港「通緝犯」的家人被滋擾、被帶走問話，這動作將會是大趨勢。二〇一九年反修例事件到現在，專業團體、公民社會一一被殲滅、取締、停刊；個人及公司資產被凍結，銀行「依足程序」把「疑犯家人」資產凍結，會否是未來趨勢？《願榮光歸香港》被律政司上訴成功，最壞情況，香港有機會「封網」，屆時香港將萬劫不復，淪為「臭港」。

在專制政權下，一國兩制變成天方夜譚。鄧小平構思的一國兩制，問題已經不是可否會真正地延續，實質上，完全被DQ了。二〇一九反送中事件至今，中國內地已經有人真正講「一國兩制」，就如以往所講的「中國夢」，信者就是真正的「發春夢」。我認識的半山熟藍絲，看到黎智英先生的處境，一間上市公司壹傳媒如此被快速「整死」，當然也感到心寒。藍友的「走資」大逃亡，並非這一兩年的事情：什麼離岸戶口、藉自己的司機、秘書開立離岸戶口，挾持他們的子女大量走資，這是極權國家借人頭外移資產的行徑，「走資」的「創意」驚人。

中國內地的白手套、流亡的「破產富豪」郭文貴曾向全世界爆料，講到中國貪官如何「走資」或把家人與情人移居澳洲，其實他提到中共「滲沙子計劃」，早已在香港發生，在沒有反對派的阻力下，暢通無阻。港人現在已在「世界的香港」從頭開始；至於香港，正在被殖民、

被換血、被溝淡。「維穩工程」會否如像西藏一樣的悲情：毀滅文化、語言及信念，大家有目共睹。

最後，前立法會議員邵家臻在一拳書店舉辦的《坐監情緒學》新書分享會，日前被國安警察上門調查，受到阻滯。根據《獨媒》報導，是接到有人舉報，分享會的讀者涉嫌參與「國安相關違規的」行為。我只可說，香港的「噤聲」行動變成日常，留下來的人，必須小心。加油！

一國兩制還可捍衛？

「世界香港論壇」在加拿大多倫多圓滿結束。中國的前榮休全國政協劉夢熊是第一位發言的嘉賓。劉和筆者，並非發夢，至今仍嘗試作「真一國兩制」的捍衛者，大聲疾呼，撥亂反正。你可能會問，一‧○鄧小平模式，現在還有嗎？中國共產黨現在給人的感覺相當不振：經濟上不振、就業前景不振、外交上，低級官員廢嗡，說到「中英聯合聲明」已成為歷史文件。

有什麼質素的人作香港「治港者」，就會有類似的效果。

李家超特首不敢正視群眾，叫大家不要再遞上請願信。我的建制半山熟之交，卻會用不同管道「上書」習近平，希望更完整地反映香港的實況：北京市西城區，西長安街，中南海中央書記處就是他的辦公室，網上可以輕易找到，沒有什麼大不了。現今的香港，很多事情，變成無稽地複雜化，令人難以理解。

二○一四年「和平佔中」之時，支持民主自由的「佔中金融組別」曾上書習近平。基本上，「上書」內容就是懇求中國共產黨根據《基本法》做事。當時的「對中國共產黨的十大訴求」，也送到「中南海」，這已經差不多是十年前的往事。然而當一國兩制已被認為變形走樣，投資者不再信任香港是法治之都，該如何走下去？

傾國家力量治理香港

筆者的金融朋友，特別是為了下一代的，都會選擇民主自由。筆者的「半山熟」建制朋友，見到香港的崩壞，經濟的下沉，其實再沒有分別什麼顏色，為求自保，也會選擇暫時離開。自「宇宙大法」實施後，已移居新加坡、英國以及美加澳紐的香港人族群為數不少。還希望在亞洲「幹一番事業」的，會落腳新加坡。

二〇二三年十一月，由 HKMA 金管局主辦的「環球金融領袖高峰會二〇二三」，Global Financial Leaders' Investment Summit（2023）再次在香港舉行。這場高峰會以前一年的經驗，算是做得不錯了。有香港政府支持，金管局主辦，主要講者食宿機票有贊助，數間大型對沖基金、投資銀行，也在名單之內。然而身邊一小撮人仍掙扎是否出席這場香港金融聚會。畢竟，港版國安法下的香港，有太多令人避之唯恐不及之處。

港版國安法和二十三條，內容其實有重疊。二十三條有兩個「環節」和「港版國安法」是互相連結的。這包括顛覆國家（sedition）及分裂國家（secession）罪行。根據特首李家超所說，二十三條立法，將會在二〇二四年內落實。二十年前，即二〇〇三年，五十萬香港人上

街，反對二十三條惡法，在香港特首董建華的年代，香港人流著汗與淚水，向政權說不。當時大家估不到二十年之後，二十三條的立法將如廣東話所說，易過「食生菜」，想來應該暢通無阻。二十三條加上港版國安法，好像嬰兒紙尿片一樣，把所有的「漏洞」塞住。二十三條加了以下重要條款：這包括叛國、外國政治團體，在香港進行政治活動、涉取國家機密、本地政治團體，與外國政治組織聯繫。至於港版國安法，有兩個款項是獨立於二十三條的：這包括恐怖活動及外國干預。

有一點很重要。全世界關注香港的人權、法治及自由，已沒有真正保障。香港的高度自治與新聞自由大開倒車。當中英聯合聲明被中方低級官員講到只是「歷史文件」；被扣押的議員、民主派人士依然失去自由之時，香港的金融中心地位，已難回復正常。君可見區議會選舉，在愛國者治港下，選出來的新一屆區議員，必然「與政府思想一致」，再沒有任何爭拗，即是這都市變得恐怖地「和諧」。

居新加坡的人，亦知新加坡並不完美；但香港的「巨變」在於，被中共以國家的力量，去「完善」任何批判聲音，實在令人難以想像香港可以再有多吸引，也將全世界對香港的信心指數，推至深淵。

世上沒有發達祕笈

對沖基金或專業投資者，不會只「低買高賣」。借貸沽空，賺到盡，就是股價跌到零。過去四份之一個世紀，跌到破產的公司，包括投資銀行雷曼兄弟、千禧年的網路玩具零售公司ETOYS。但在了解市場脈動的同時，我們也必須知道，任何基本分析或技術分析，都難以「神準」。

沒有需求的股票，市場只有沽貨，股票可以跌到好殘。大型對沖基金沽空，一個投資網站發起「護盤」行為，結果變了散戶與及投資大鱷的投資爭霸戰。兩年前，小投資者把蚊型公司炒上，很多也是如此概念。加拿大的大麻股，數年前便是炒賣的對象。

近年，北美市場，遊戲軟體公司 Game Stop 曾經成為投資人的熱話。Game Stop 的管理層在二〇二一年做出大幅轉變，換了新的 CEO Ryan Cohen。這位年近四十歲、從未讀過大學的加拿大、猶太裔商業奇才，早年創辦了網上寵物食品公司 Chewy。在二〇一七年，他集資三億五千萬美元之後上市。二〇一七年四月，Pet smart 收購了 Chewy，動用資金為三十三・五億美元。他也累積了更大的財富。大家不可不知，Ryan Cohen 也是蘋果的前三位最大單一股東之一。

市場是零和遊戲，傳統基金的做法又不同。有些在招股書中，會介紹基金經理的策略，如何揀股，什麼類別，會否善用正股，可否作 covered call，這些相對上是保守策略。來到對沖基金的領域，以技巧為本的策略，絕對更廣更闊。

一念天堂一念地獄，在絕對回報的領域，散戶捍衛戰，在波幅的大市，其實就是要做到力保不失。投資大型對沖基金的，並非「輸得起」，而是希望有相對較高的回報。在現在高利率的情況下（美元存款也超過百分之五），利率繼續有機會攀升，又何必放入資本市場？

一位中年人，窮一生精力，可能儲蓄到三百萬美元。假若此君是單身人士，住在一個高消費的城市，例如舊金山，又假如他沒有物業，是在矽谷「被淘汰」的六十歲高科技行政人員，其實他可能「幾頭痛」。又假如他在南部德州，情況又很不同。

最後，富貴如浮雲。也有百億美元身家的中國共產黨員，用權力賺取金錢，用灰色地帶的途徑把資金運去海外，卻被世界第一大黨「越洋追凶」。這其實就是要拿你的血汗錢，畢竟他們是貪婪與權力的佼佼者。希望大家明白，長線投資的一大道理便是：不努力而得之財，必然消耗；勤勞積蓄的，必然增加。祝君好運！

APEC峰會，世界在看

在美國舊金山舉行的 APEC 亞太經貿會議，坦白說，並非「改變世界」的最大會議。習近平和拜登的舊金山會面得到什麼結局難料。美國兩會敦促總統拜登和習近平會議之時，可以拿出一個「香港及中國政治犯名單」，給習近平「考慮」之用。

美國現中國為商業上最強競爭對手，而政治考量上，也是強力的競爭對手。中國、俄羅斯、北韓及伊朗，被現今自由世界形容為「邪惡核心」，對與錯，大家心裡有數。當烏克蘭和俄羅斯繼續戰爭，世界的焦點現在又放入色列與哈馬斯的戰爭中。

APEC 議程當中，也加入了 APEC 的 CEO 聚會，希望製造商業機會，創造無限可能。其實，現實世界當中，新加坡、臺灣、越南及柬埔寨也成為中國的競爭對手。而預計二〇二四，並沒有「世界第三次大戰」，只有更複雜的政治博弈。

再談 APEC 一些花邊新聞。與習近平在舊金山「同枱食飯」要四千美元，而「經濟客位」，卻要二千美元。HKDC 行政總監郭鳳儀以及八九六四民運領袖王丹，在習訪美期間，舉辦了各類型的抗議活動，而「小粉紅」則有更大的資源歡迎習近平。對美國而言，中國和俄羅斯，是

隨時引爆第三次世界大戰的「元凶」；所以「香港議題」在APEC峰會當中並不是著眼點。

故，若期待香港政治犯的現狀因為APEC峰會而有所改變（如「放人」保外就醫），近乎不可能。「宇宙大法」預計會重判曾經為香港自由無限付出的朋友；香港人關心的政治人物，如黎智英、鄒幸彤及黃之鋒等人，仍然會長時間被扣留。還是這一句：願上主憐憫香港的義人！

年尾收爐，命運在手

這天是二○二三年各大交易所的最後交易日。香港交易所（388）股票，二○二三年下跌近百分之二十四，相當之嚇人。美國三大指數：道瓊斯、納斯達克、標普500指數，在加息周期下，整個二○二三年，走勢波動，但過關斬將；而道指及標普在歷史高位徘徊。

股市大行情永遠難捉摸，科技股走勢過關斬將，一步一驚心。微軟（MSFT）、亞馬遜（AMZN）、蘋果（AAPL）及谷歌（GOOG）早已破萬億美元市值；而Nvidia（NVDA）在二○二三年六月，也成功成為萬億美元市值公司。過去三年，用二○二一年第一個交易日計算，Nvidia上升了百分之兩百，現時市值約為一點二萬億美元。至於娛樂事業巨人，如迪士尼及串樓媒體公司Netflix，值得注意的是迪士尼的市值要比Netflix低，前者市值為一千六百五十四億，後者為兩千一百五十億。

加拿大皇家銀行RBC收購匯豐加拿大已獲批准，二○二四年第一季估計收購完成，如何把加拿大的HSBC融入RBC，日後將會逐漸揭曉。現在更大的問題是，假如在加拿大匯豐做了定期存款，如何把整個定息存款Roll Over到RBC；匯豐的環球Globex匯豐，是否到二○二四年

第一季末完結，這些需要交代。香港很多人用 HSBC，而移民來加的港人更相信這品牌。近年匯豐的爭議相當大，包括凍結了「港版國安法」指令下的個人及公司資產。加拿大匯豐將會變成「歷史」，相對於一些港人和香港銀行有 clean break 的，未嘗不是一件壞事。

加密貨幣交易平台倒閉，也是二〇二三年的大事。較為年輕的朋友，一定對區塊鏈交易平台 FTX 宣布破產極為驚訝。FTX 的創辦人 Sam Bankman-Fried（簡寫SBF）二〇一九年在香港成立了一個名為 FTX 的加密衍生工具交易所。長話短說，這位麻省理工 MIT 物理學畢業生，曾在坐盤交易商 Jane Street 工作，後來創業。劇情發展到現在，FTX 這個區塊鏈交易平台正式宣佈倒閉，創辦人 Sam 由在巴哈馬群島「穩居」後，被美國政府遣返受審。FTX 曾經管理過千億資產，而 Sam Bankman-Fried 預計將在二〇二四年初獲最終法院判決。另一邊廂，同樣值得留意的是，Binance 幣安執行長趙長鵬明年可能要入獄，反洗錢指控認罪，雖然他與幣安和美國政府達成全面和解協議，允許該加密貨幣交易所得以繼續運營。

最後，市場人士估計，二〇二四年美國或有減息機會，而在絕對回報的領域，長短均可。要做一個「刀槍不入」的主力倉，其實就是要把「資金曲線」一路推上，尋求絕對「正回報」。如果息率繼續膨脹，當然定期存款在某種程度上更加吸引。還是給大家十六字真言，在我的操作字典內，永久長青：「順勢而行、長短均可、風險控制、量力而為。」每個人都應該為自己做好準備，做一個紮實的「主力倉」，走到最後。

香港大崩壞，自由價更高

美國政府可能通過的「香港制裁法案」，針對「港版國安法」下美國認為損害香港核心價值的香港持份者，包括國安法法官及檢控官，作出應有的制裁與懲罰。不能在香港開銀行戶口，這只是其中一個範疇。整條法案尚未通過，英文名稱叫 Hong Kong Sanctions Act。現在美國的姿態，就是對沖現在他們認為香港的司法制度的崩壞。是否具很大意義？

過去十多年間，筆者在香港出版了十本時事加投資元素的書籍。直至二○一九年香港反修例事件、二○二○年「港版國安法」實施後，因香港的政治巨變，再沒有可能出版「講真話」的書了。香港的「一國兩制」，在中共不守承諾的情況下，五十年不變，近乎已成為了全廢話。筆者在二○一九年七月，最後的香港著作是「致富活著三」，而三本著作，即《致富活著1、2、3》，居然在香港圖書館成了「禁書」。理由？我們支持「真的一國兩制」，普選是終極目標；是其是、非其非，這樣也要「禁」。往後的連鎖效應：香港的金融資產，正在退場中，因治港者「真的搞壞了香港」。在「愛國者治港」的年代，香港出現了「倒退一百五十年」的現象；曾經的英國殖民地給予香港的優良基石，現在卻是一一擦掉。

二〇二三年也快完結，而二〇二四年將會是巨變之年。有幸和臺灣出版社合作，藉由文字的力量，盼將歷史傳承。寶島的自由得來不易，而在大部份香港人的眼裡，臺灣早已是「臺灣」：有自由、法治、投票權以及公民權利。一九四九年，國民黨敗走臺灣，這是不爭的歷史，臺灣政黨，百花齊放。而中共建議和臺灣的「一國兩制」，其實凶險萬分。臺海維持現狀，可能是最好的方法。

本年也快完結，美國三大指數：道瓊斯、納斯達克、標普500指數，在整個二〇二三年，走勢依舊強勁，但也極為波動。股市大行情永遠相對容易捉摸，而科技股走勢則過關斬將，一步一驚心。微軟（MSFT）、亞馬遜（AMZN）、蘋果（AAPL）及谷歌（GOOG）早已破萬億美元市值，而Nvidia（NVDA），在二〇二三年六月，也成功成為萬億美元市值的公司，創辦人黃仁勳，本身便是美籍的臺灣人。

筆者正在筆耕，希望在臺灣總統大選前後完成的本書，帶讀者前往另一想像空間：不單只著重投資回報，更要關注世界的事情，注重「人生回報」。在這本小書中，我們從四年前說起，即二〇一九年。

回顧二〇一九年，是中國建政七十週年、西藏抗暴六十週年、八九六四屠城三十週年，也是香港多事之秋的一年。二〇一九年農曆新年過後，香港的《逃犯條例》修訂建議，這「政治

核彈」，轟爆香港原有的核心價值。「光時」，以及「願榮光」，把跨世代的香港人團結一起，說到底便是「獅子山下」的精神。

時光「快閃」到如今二〇二三年的最後倒數。香港人為了逃避共產黨，到處漂泊，部份落腳臺灣、英美加澳紐等地。香港人不懂政治，但政治始終要埋身。而自二〇二二年起，世界聚焦俄羅斯及烏克蘭；二〇二三年恐怖組織哈馬斯突襲以色列，中東局勢以致全世界的和平穩定都亮起了警號。未來美中長久的政治博弈將如何發展，前總統川普是否重返白宮，都是「未知數」。

我沒有水晶球。但願二〇二四年，臺灣選出的新總統能為亞洲以至全世界帶來很好的示範：小國能做超乎想像的大事。

最後，返回金融的領域。「絕對回報」是鬥智鬥力的遊戲，我喜愛參與其中。但坦白說，十年如一日的投資生涯，真是沒有多大意義，特別是當我進入了人生下半場的「上場」之後，我更加有這種強烈感覺。五十知天命，這個「死線」，五年多前，已順利降臨到筆者身上，很多事情從頭開始。金融操盤原本是我的主軸，但香港巨變，最有能力的人身陷獄中，筆者唯有待他們「發聲」，在世界各地，繼續說香港的真正故事。

2014年雨傘運動後，有幾年時間，紀念9.28這個日子，直至2019年反修例事件。

上｜2017年山頂區議會補選，當中幫忙「打氣」的譚文豪、胡志偉、毛孟靜及楊岳橋，全因港版國安法而被扣押，香港民主大倒退。

下｜2017年區議會選舉補選，挑戰的是「贏不到」的山頂區，但依然參與，務求建制派不能「自動當選」。

上｜和戴耀廷教授及毛孟靜在中環，繼續追求民主理念發聲。
左下｜戴耀廷教授是拔萃男書院的學兄，多謝他無條件的付出。
右下｜認識黎智英先生超過30年，他為香港人付出了一切。

上｜與李柱銘三十年前的合照。
左下｜李柱銘是香港民主之父，在國安法下，也被噤聲。
右下｜郭家麒醫生因參與初選，已被扣押接近三年時間。

上｜陶傑是香江才子，現已移居英國。
左中｜在香港與末代港督彭定康，在他的新
　　　書發佈會碰面。
右中｜馮智活牧師是香港回歸前的立法會議
　　　員。
　下｜陳日君樞機是我敬重的人物，奉獻一
　　　生於真道。

上｜郭卓堅先生，與
　　筆者認識多年，
　　他的綽號是長洲
　　司法覆核王。
中｜鄒幸彤是支聯會
　　副主席及香港的
　　大律師，現在跟
　　港版國安化下，
　　已被扣押。
下｜筆者與黃之鋒、
　　周庭。

上 | 最後一次返大陸，應該是2017年的年尾。當時還未有「被送中」這議題。
下 | 如今，港島區中環，人和事已急速地變。

上｜離開香港前三個月，領養了的唐狗Eevee。
左下｜2021年六月尾，離開香港時心情複雜，不知下次何時再返香港。
右下｜2021年六月尾，離開香港後一個月，和友人宋先生在溫哥華報導，正式離開
　　　香港，海外暫居。

上｜接受財經頻道CNBC訪問，談到一
　　國兩制是否仍存在。
左中｜出席歐洲人權會議，談到香港一國
　　　兩制的崩壞。
右中｜與吾爾開希一起出席人權會議。
左下｜2023年尾在芝加哥Urban Voice教
　　　會作分享。

2019年反修例事件，喚醒了香港人。